Pebbles

Pebbles

Memories of a
Small-Town Kansas Boy

Gary White

To Elyn—beloved partner, friend, confidant, travel companion, and body buddy.

Pebbles
Memories of a Small-Town Kansas Boy

by Gary White

Copyright © 2008 by Pilgrims Process, Inc.

Set in Minion Pro 11 pt. with
Stone Sans Bold in various sizes for display

ISBN: 978-0-9790909-7-4

Library of Congress Control Number:

2008930221

Printed in the United States of America

0 9 8 7 6 5 4 3 2 1

Contents

Forward

These short fragments are drawn from the actual experience of my life as I remember it, having rolled around in my memory over the years. Like pebbles in a stream, most of these little pieces have been rounded and polished by frequent retelling. In fact, the only requirement for inclusion in this collection is that I have retold these stories so many times that they have been polished to the highest sheen that they are likely to have. Over the process of years these stories have been shaped by my personal telephone effect. As a child, you probably played the telephone game. You are told a few sentences, and then you tell it to another person, and they tell it to a third, until a whole group has participated and you can compare how little the final version resembles the original. In a similar way, I hear myself telling these stories and then repeating them with slight variations until their relationship to the original experience has become somewhat tenuous. They have been filtered many times through my imperfect memory.

I have no grand purpose in retelling these stories—no sermons to deliver, no scheme to save the world. I do have a well-formed "philosophy" that I live by and that philosophy is bound to emerge in the stories. It has not been laboriously worked out or instilled by moral authority; it is simply the result of my life experiences. This "philosophy" has seen me through seventy-plus years, and I have emerged with no more than the usual scars and abrasions. I say this so you won't expect to be enlightened or edified by reading these little pieces. They are just what they are: small nuggets drawn from a lifetime of experience.

If you are still with me after these disclaimers, you are a candidate for dipping into *Pebbles*. There is a very simple organization to this book, so you can open it to any section and read a piece. Because I have applied the organization that emerges if you take a bucket full of pebbles and shake them you won't miss any critical information by skipping around. The larger pieces tend to be near the front of the book and the shorter pieces later. In a few cases I have grouped a series of pieces together because of similar content.

This method of organizing a book has a long and distinguished history. The *Koran*, the sacred scripture of Islam, is organized from shortest to longest chapter with no recognizable connection between the subject matter of the neighboring *suras*. I took the *Koran* as a fine model (in reverse) for going about the organization of *Pebbles*. If you are wanting something short, go toward the end; if you want something a little longer, choose accordingly.

Early versions of some of these stories have been shared with members of my high school classes in Cedar Vale, Kansas. A group of us have maintained an internet blog where we can share our memories with each other. (See www.CedarValeMemories.blogspot.com.) Most of my stories about Cedar Vale have been published on this blog, and my classmates have in some cases amplified my memories by adding significant details. I have included these in the stories, much as bits of contrasting stone are included in conglomerate rocks. I have made no attempt to identify the specific bits that belong to my classmates, but Wayne Woodruff, Don Cox, Phil Foust, T. D. Oltjen, and Reva Sawyer have all contributed to my Cedar Vale stories. I hereby acknowledge my debt to them for jogging my memory of the earlier days.

For anyone who didn't grow up with me, I will tell you that I was born in rural southern Kansas in 1937, moving to Cedar Vale, Kansas, when I was around three years of age. I lived in Cedar Vale until I began college at The University of Kansas in 1955. I have three music degrees from KU and a Ph.D. in Music Composition from Michigan State University. I taught at Iowa State University for twenty-eight years, retiring in 1994. Since that time, my second wife, Elyn, and I have lived in Colorado, Spain, France, and most recently, Santa Fe, New Mexico.

Two things remain to be said. In a few cases, other living persons might be embarrassed by what I write, so I have substituted fictitious names and made judicious changes in details. Most other names and places are real. Secondly, some of these stories may embarrass *you* due to my frank approach to subjects such as sex. I warn you in advance.

The inspiration for *Pebbles* came during a recent trip to Ireland, when I found myself retelling some of these stories to people who asked about my life. On this tour of sacred sites in the Emerald Isle I experienced an evening shamanic journey to the Cailleach (sometimes known as the Old Hag), one of the ancestral goddesses of the land. In an evening of intense shamanic drumming led by Martin Duffy, director of the Irish Centre for Shamanic Studies, we were placed in direct contact with this ancient earth goddess. I asked the Cailleach for advice on how to go about writing this book, and her response was quite direct and simple: "No bullshit." I've taken her at her word and have written as close to the unvarnished truth about my life as my memory allows.

If you have an interest in small-town midwestern life in the 1940s and 50s or are simply curious about the details of my life, you may find this book of interest. Also, my children may be interested in some of these details of their father's life, family, and times.

Now you know as much as I do about the genesis of *Pebbles*. I wish you a pleasant journey as you began to pluck some stones from the stream of my memory.

Leonard Theater, Cedar Vale, Kansas

Movies were the principal form of entertainment in Cedar Vale, Kansas, in the late 1940s, before the advent of television in the area. The Leonard Theater did a brisk business, showing three different movies each week: a western or other action film on Friday and Saturday; a good clean family movie, such as a musical or a comedy, on Sunday, Monday, and Tuesday; and a serious drama or thriller on Wednesday and Thursday. (The Wednesday and Thursday fare were often what is now called "film noir" by film buffs.) I attended at least once each week and twice if there was something good on. Admission was $.25 for kids. My 50-cent allowance would stretch to two movies per week if I didn't spend some of it at the drug store.

The theater on Main Street had been a small vaudeville or "opera" house in earlier days. It had a full proscenium-arch stage and seated about 200 patrons on one floor, which was ample for the 900 or so people living in Cedar Vale at the time. The front entrance of the theater was recessed off the sidewalk and had four steps leading up to the ticket booth in the center, with swinging doors on either side. At the left side of this area was Bill Leonard's office, which looked out on the entrance through a series of windows.

Bill and Maude Leonard owned the theater. Bill was the chief projectionist and Maude sold tickets. I seldom saw Maude except when she was seated in the ticket booth, wearing a felt hat or turban and heavy makeup. Maude always reminded me of a gypsy fortune teller, with her colorful costumes that were often made of some form of velvet. She may have really been on the show circuit, along with Bill. Bill was long, lean, and stooped. He worked in his office in the hour before the start of the movie at 7:00 p.m. I would stop by to visit with him before watching the movie, and he would regale me with stories of his days in the circus band or on tour with various shows. We became the best of friends.

Bill had been a musician, the first professional musician I ever met. His office had musical instruments hanging on the walls, along with posters from the great movies he had shown at the theater over the years.

It was rumored around town that Maude had been a show girl, and the couple was thought to be "not quite" respectable by the more straight-laced population of the town. If Maude had been on the vaudeville stage, it hadn't been for many years, because they were both up in years by the time I knew them. Bill was clearly in ill health. He was very thin, with the constant cough of a consumptive. Maude was not in much better shape, but a heavy coating of makeup covered the worst of the ravages of time. Stories circulating in Cedar Vale about Maude Leonard included a rumor that she had hoarded bushel baskets filled with dimes collected from the receipts of the theater and that she was known to shoplift from the grocery stores she shopped in. A classmate who worked for the grocery department at L. C. Adam Mercantile reports that Maude helped herself quite liberally to the fresh produce, devastating the grapes and other small fruit.

Bill sat in his office chair, looking as if he might not be able to summon the energy to make the nightly climb to the projection booth. He had a long basset-hound face and the largest ears I had ever seen. His doleful eyes would light up only when speaking of his past glories, and then he would become quite animated and laugh at the various adventures and misadventures he had lived through. I thought that the life of a musician on the road must be about the most exciting thing imaginable, and I dreamed of someday playing with a circus band. As a sixth grader, I had just started lessons on the trumpet, and Bill's stories sent me home to practice even harder to make the high school band and someday "go on the road."

Bill's office work consisted of booking future films and preparing the ads that were shown before the cartoon each evening. The theater had a magic-lantern slide projector that used three-by-five-inch glass slides. Bill would paint the ads directly on these glass slides, using a white opaque paint. He was the local sign painter in the daytime (another skill learned in the circus, I imagined), and his ads were carefully lettered and even sported simple artwork in the form of stick figures in various amusing poses that illustrated the content of the ad. He would often be painting when I arrived, and I would wait in silence while he finished so I wouldn't distract him and cause him to make a mistake.

As our friendship deepened, I started going to his office even on evenings when I wasn't going to the movie. I would spend some time with Bill and then move on up the block to talk with Mrs. Walker, the owner of Whitney Drug Store (See "Whitney Drug Store," p. 36). One evening when I stopped by, having already seen the current movie, Bill asked if I would like to join him in the projection booth. I was immediately excited, and he took me up to show me around before the film started. The projection balcony was directly over the office and entrance area, up one flight of stairs. You had to go in the main entrance of the theater to reach this set of stairs, which were hidden behind a door in the lobby.

The projection balcony was divided into two areas, one containing the projection machines and another where Bill could sit when he was not having to change the film in one of the projectors. The projectors contained open carbon arcs that burned white hot, so that the projection room was always stifling. The light for the projectors was obtained by the electric arc between two round carbon rods about five inches in length. The rods were gradually consumed inside the projectors, which were vented through the ceiling. Keeping them adjusted for maximum light was a frequent job. The room contained two movie projectors and the magic lantern. Along the back wall was a machine for rewinding and splicing film, and the whole room was heavily padded to keep the sound of the projectors from disturbing the patrons. The current film was in large reels in metal cases stacked on the floor. In the small sitting area outside there were two huge turntables that had been used to play the sound track for early talking films, before the days when the sound track was placed directly on the film. One of these turntables was used to play records in the minutes before the film began and during the showing of the magic-lantern ads.

Bill showed me how he threaded the projectors and adjusted the carbon arcs. At the beginning of the evening he would load both projectors before starting the magic-lantern slides. Then he would start playing a 78-rpm record and go to the booth to show the slides. On the wall between the projectors was a three-way switch that would shift the sound system from the records over to either of the projectors. Bill would run through his slides and then move to the first projector. He would start the projector and when the film sound began, throw the sound switch and at the same time operate a shutter that cut off the light from the magic lantern and opened the projection hole for the first projector. If his timing was perfect, there would be a smooth segue into the film. Then he shut down the magic lantern, and he was free to rest in the sitting area until the first reel ran out.

Near the end of a reel of film there are a series of warning spots on the upper right corner of the film. Bill would start the second projector precisely on one of the warning dots and then switch both the sound and the shutter in front of the projectors at the same time. If his timing was good there was scarcely any discontinuity in the projected image or sound. Then he would remove the reel from the first projector and place it on the rewinding machine while he reloaded that projector. There was a separate reel for the preview of coming attractions and the cartoon.

Most films were "three-reelers," so Bill had to reload each projector only once in an evening. Of course, if the film broke or a projector jammed, he could be called into service on a moments notice. Otherwise he rested in an overstuffed chair in the sitting area, periodically checking to see if the carbon arcs were OK. If there was a technical difficulty, all the kids and some of the adults in the theater below would stamp their feet and make other disrespectful noises, and Bill would have to work at double speed to mend the problem. I thought Bill's profession was quite glamorous. He was still in the entertainment business, just as he had been in earlier years.

After that first visit to the projection booth, I became a regular. I would first have to pay and see the current feature, then Maude would let me in free the next night to visit with Bill. This ensured that they weren't giving out free passes. For a few years I spent one or two evenings each week sitting with Bill in that cramped little sitting room or following him around as he operated the projectors. I saw various projection disasters, such as film jams that ate up several feet of film and the burnout of the carbon arcs in the middle of a reel. When a carbon arc burned out, Bill would have to stop the show and replace the carbon electrodes. This was dangerous work because of the high voltages and high temperatures involved. The patrons would clap, stamp and whistle all the time that Bill was working feverishly inside the projector. I heard a lot about what he thought of his patrons during those emergencies!

When I entered the upper grades, I spent less and less time with Bill at the theater. I began to go to the movies with friends, and activities at the school occupied more and more of my time. I didn't realize that Bill's health was deteriorating badly until I heard one day that he had died. This came as a real shock to me.

Mr. Beggs (my high-school band director) asked me to join him and Tommy Gordon to form a trumpet trio to play hymns for Bill Leonard's funeral. We wore our band uniforms for this event, which was staged in the movie theater. The preacher, Rev. Goss of the Assembly of God Church, was up on stage in front of the screen and Bill's coffin was in the lobby. We set up our music stands in an open area near one of the fire exits at the front of the auditorium. I don't remember many details of the funeral, but it was somehow both a solemn and a festive affair. Our trumpet trio played several hymns and some of the townspeople spoke.

As we filed out of the theater past Bill's open coffin, we saw that he had been dressed in his band uniform, with gold braid and brass buttons down the front. The trumpet trio accompanied the funeral procession to the cemetery, where Bill was laid to rest accompanied by hymns. I remember feeling that, if we had only brought some drums, we could have formed a Dixieland band to play a rousing version of "When the Saints Go Marching In" as we left the cemetery. I know that Bill would have liked that a lot. I think it was altogether one of the most appropriate funerals I have ever attended.

That funeral marked the end of an era in Cedar Vale. The Leonard Theater was no more. Maude Leonard went to live with a niece or a daughter in Kansas City. Several years later, when I was a senior at the University of Kansas, this woman contacted me to let me know the Maude had died and that there were some of Bill's items that she had wanted me to have. I drove to Kansas City and spent an evening with her, talking of Bill and Maude. She gave me Bill's cornet, clarinet, and a derby hat, which are the most tangible artifacts of my childhood and youth in Cedar Vale, Kansas. The instruments were old and unplayable, but I enjoyed wearing the derby hat from time to time.

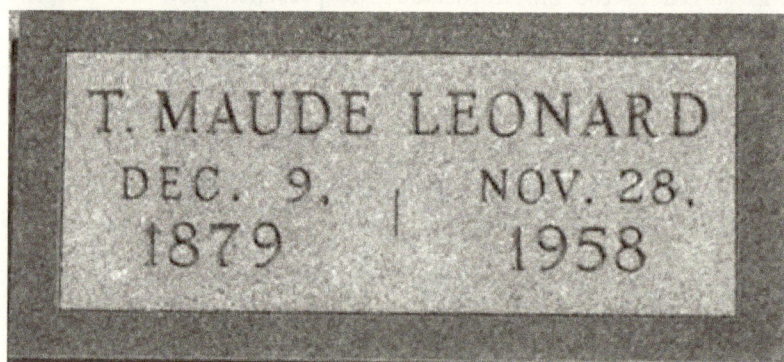

Bill Leonard
(1881-1952)

In the previous piece on the Leonard Theater I related what I knew or thought I knew of Bill Leonard, who was my friend when I was a young boy growing up in Cedar Vale, Kansas. Now I'll tell you what I learned from subsequent research, which includes extensive searching of census records and a copy of Bill's obituary, which Don Cox generously provided.

William W. (Bill) Leonard was born on July 20, 1881, in Waterloo, Iowa, the son of John E. Leonard and Margaret (Maggie) Leonard. His father was a railroad brakeman. When John died shortly after 1885, Maggie took Bill and his older brother, Charley, to Lebanon, in north-central Kansas, where she married an older man, Seneca S. Lake, and the boys grew to manhood. In the 1900 US Census eighteen-year-old Bill is listed as an apprentice painter and twenty-year-old Charley is clerking in the post office.

According to his obituary, Bill was very active as a trombone and tuba player in the local band, which was led by Charley. Sometime later, Bill established a drugstore in Lebanon. Apparently, a degree in pharmacy was not a requirement for dispensing medicines at the turn of the century in Kansas.

In Lebanon, Bill met and married T. Maude Pennington (1879-1958), who had a daughter, or perhaps a niece, Mona B. White. The couple took Mona as their daughter and they moved to Cedar Vale in November of 1907, where they purchased a half interest in Pattison Drug Store. This store, which was originally known as Pattison and Leonard, became Leonard's Drug Store when Bill purchased the interest of his partner. Bill and Maude operated this drugstore in Cedar Vale for thirty-one years.

The Leonard Drug Store featured a soda fountain with the standard marble counter and high revolving stools permanently mounted to the floor. The back bar was also of marble, and there were large mirrors with glass jars of colored liquid for decoration, like most other soda fountains of the day. The non-standard item was a large sign on the wall above the mirror, which read: "Freeze your lips, ice your teeth, and give your tongue a sleigh ride." This was, of course, the work of Bill and carried the usual "Bill done it" in a lower corner. Maude would often mix up the ingredients for sherbets and ice creams, which were frozen using an old-fashioned hand-cranked ice-cream freezer.

In the back there were display cases for patent medicines and other over-the-counter drugs, along with bottles of Bill's own patent medicine, which he called "Cee Vee Healing Oil" and labeled "recommended for both man and beast." A correspondent from Cedar Vale relates that he often helped Bill concoct the mixture, twenty gallons at a time. It was sold in the store and also exported to the surrounding areas, where it was a popular product.

Along with his work in the drug store and the theater, Bill continued his interest in music, organizing and directing The Girls Band (see photo on p. 43), The Men's Band, Alexander's Ragtime Band, and The Hobo Band, which gained considerable regional fame in southeastern Kansas. He also took over the Old Opera House in Cedar Vale, where he presented local talent shows along with road and stage shows that passed through the area. He brought carnivals and tent shows, called Chautauquas after their place of origin in Chautauqua, New York, to Cedar Vale. I don't know what, if any, relationship exists between Chautauqua County, Kansas, and Chautauqua, New York.

The Old Opera House continued until the advent of motion pictures. When movies became a national phenomenon in the 1930s Bill and Maude opened the Mystic Theatre, the first movie theater in

Cedar Vale, on the site where Herb's Cafe later stood. I well remember that in back of Herb's joint were the remains of this earlier building, which may have been razed or perhaps burned down.

Bill published a small newspaper called "Mystic Murmurs" for seven years while he was the proprietor of the Mystic Theatre. If you have the impression of a man who was constantly on the move, consider that Bill was also the local sign painter during all those years. His signs were in evidence all over Cedar Vale, each with the characteristic signature "Bill done it" on the lower corner. I remember that many of Bill's signs were displayed all over town at the time of his death on November 28, 1952.

Bill and Maude took over another theater (the Princess Theatre) on a main street site next to the bank and brought the name Mystic Theatre over to it. Later this became the Leonard Theater and sported a large sign painted by Bill over the entrance. This is the site of all my early adventures with Bill and the movies that I have previously described.

Sometime in the 1930s the Leonards sold the drug store to Don Hankins, who was operating the store as a standard drug store and pharmacy when I was growing up in Cedar Vale.

While Bill Leonard was not the widely traveled professional touring musician or circus musician I imagined him to be from the many tales he told me when I visited him in his office or projection booth, he was a natural showman of great local fame in Chautauqua County, Kansas. Bill and Maude were responsible for much of the cultural life of Cedar Vale during the first half of the twentieth century. In Bill's obituary the writer says, "A book could be written about Bill for his life was an open book. His ever outstanding sunny smile, good manners, and love for all, especially his love for children and animals, will always be remembered, not by one but by all." This short piece along with my piece on the Leonard Theater will have to stand as my humble attempt to write chapters for that book.

"In a Little Spanish Town . . ."

So go the lyrics of a popular song from my youth. I actually had the opportunity to live out that dream in 1997, after Elyn and I were married. Elyn had done the research for her Ph.D. in cultural anthropology in Spain. Her topic and her passion was the Camino de Santiago, a 500-mile-long 1000-year-old pilgrimage road that crosses the Pyrenees from France and then stretches from east to west across the northern part of Spain. We traveled there in the summer of 1996 and I met the family who had become her Spanish family when she was living in Spain and walking the Camino. I had always wanted to live in a foreign country long enough to move beyond tourist status, and this looked like the perfect opportunity. Elyn's Spanish family invited us to come back to Sahagún and live, so in the summer of 1997 we packed up our things, sold the rest of them, and moved to Spain to live in Europe for a few years.

First we walked the Camino, just as Elyn had done in 1982 when she was doing her dissertation research. Then we moved into the furnished apartment that our Spanish family had found for us above a hardware store in downtown Sahagún in north-central Spain, a small town of 2500 people. The apartment was luxurious by any standard and cost us a fraction of what we would spend in the U.S. for similar accommodations. My Spanish was nearly nonexistent, since I had forgotten all of my high-school Spanish, but Elyn was quite fluent and I was willing to learn.

Living as a resident in another country is much different than being a tourist. We had to negotiate such necessities as getting phone service, getting internet connections, the post office, the bank, grocery shopping, etc. In all these areas our Spanish family was more than helpful, and in short order we were firmly established in town. Elyn's language ability ensured that everything worked smoothly.

Our apartment had been decorated by the owner of the hardware store below. By Spanish standards he was an accomplished interior decorator. We had heavy Spanish furniture, an elaborate crystal chandelier above the huge dining table and chairs, walls that had many coats of sparkly, textured finish on them, and the standard metal-blind window coverings *(persianas)* that most Spanish houses have to protect them from the heat of the afternoon sun. There were balconies in the front and the back overlooking eleventh-century churches and the bustling downtown area, and we had two faux-marble-tiled luxurious bathrooms with the latest fixtures. The kitchen had a dishwasher and a clothes washer of the latest design, along with complete sets of dishes, glassware, silverware, and cooking utensils. We only needed to unpack our personal items to be completely at home.

Our Spanish family, the Luna-Tovars, took us in, just as they had Elyn many years before. We were invited to all the family dinners and outings. If we didn't appear daily at the little bookstore and souvenir shop that had been in the family for two generations, Paca, the matriarch of the family, would appear at our door and exclaim, "Have you died?" Not only were we welcomed into the family, we also had family obligations to fulfill.

At first the novelty of everything kept me totally entranced. Grocery shopping was a new experience. There was the shop to go to that had the best meat, another for fish, a third for fruits and vegetables, and a small supermarket for the household supplies that we needed. Paca told us where to shop for the best deals, and we would move through the town accumulating what we needed in string grocery bags.

Sahagún was the municipal center for the surrounding region—rather like a county seat. Every Saturday there was an open air market in the streets below our apartment. There we could get nearly everything we wanted, from inexpensive clothing to freshly rotisseried chickens. The streets filled with people from the surrounding areas, and there was much pushing and shouting as people vied with each other for the attention of the sellers. One thing that became very obvious to me immediately was just how loud the Spanish people are. They seem to all talk at the same time and to shout at each other. At first I thought they might be angry, but then I realized that "loud" is just their way of being in the world. Soon I could push and shout with the best of them (besides, I was a lot taller!), and every Saturday was a lot of fun and excitement.

On Sundays we were expected to attend the Luna-Tovar's family dinner. These dinners would start in the early afternoon and extend through the evening hours. There were seldom fewer than a dozen people in attendance and, just as on the streets, everyone talked at the same time in loud voices. There was much joking among the family and I took my share of the jibes, even though I was not good at retaliating. Much was made of my great size (with considerable inuendo concerning my large feet) and, indeed, I was taller by far than any member of the family. In fact, I was nearly the tallest person in Sahagún.

The food was plentiful and we were expected to eat generous quantities. Lamb that had been roasted to perfection with olive oil, salt, and garlic in the wood-burning oven was absolutely heavenly, and a large variety of vegetables were prepared with Paca's expert hand. The family made its own wine (we even helped stomp the grapes), which was served in generous quantities, and they had hams that had been salted and dried in the attic. Paca was a master chef who could prepare the *tortilla española* (a potato, onion, and egg pie) and bake the best flan I ever tasted. In the middle of the afternoon there was usually a lull in activity when everyone took a short siesta or played cards, but later on the family began to gather to eat again from the leftovers of dinner and the party was on again in full force.

I was totally unprepared for the rhythm of Spanish life. Spaniards usually get a rather slow start on the day and arrive around 9:00 a.m.

at work after having little or no breakfast, perhaps some bread and jam. They eat several small snacks during the early part of the day and close up shop at around 2:00 p.m. to go home for the afternoon siesta. Lunch, which is usually the largest meal of the day, would be served at around 3 p.m., followed by a quiet time or even a nap. They would then return to work at 5:00 or 6:00 p.m. Shops would open again and remain open until around 8:00 p.m. Then it was time for a light dinner before the evening activities began. People came out on the streets of Sahagún *en mass* in the evening.

A typical evening would start with *un paseo,* a walk outside of town with conversations with neighbors and friends. Then the town square would fill with families. The adults would drink, play games, and socialize while the children ran and played together on the plaza. Just when I would think it was time to go home, the real evening activities would begin. On weekends, bars and night clubs would open around 11:00 p.m. Drinking and dancing went on until 3:00 or 4:00 a.m. The hours for sleeping were short. When we complained that we needed to go home to sleep, we were told, "The more you sleep, the less you live!" We quickly became known as "sleepy heads" and our family teased us unmercifully for our American habits.

We were very happy in our little Spanish town until, in the spring, we began to feel a subtle oppression. Spain is a country that has known much oppression. Spaniards were oppressed by the Spanish Inquisition, beginning in 1478, which ruthlessly stamped out all religious diversity and ran the Jews and the Moors out of Spain in 1492, after executing many thousands of them. The Inquisition was supplemented by other dictatorships over the centuries, then by an equally ruthless fascist state run by Generalissimo Franco. The country only emerged as a democracy in the mid-1970s, and many vestiges of both the Inquisition and fascism still exist. There is a national police force, the *Guardia Civil,* created by Franco, that still remains a heavy-handed presence in every small town. The Catholic Church was aligned with the fascist government and continues to exert itself in all areas of Spanish life. This is not a country that tolerates much diversity. We began to feel the subtle oppression, even though we were tolerated as outsiders and our Spanish family treated us with great love and affection. We began to wish to breathe freer air. We knew that our time in Spain was nearly over.

We decided to move to France, a country we had visited several times during our stay in Spain. The sudden illness and death of both of our mothers changed our plans. In August 1998 we found ourselves on our way back to the U.S. I had achieved my goal of living in a foreign country long enough to not be a tourist, and I was happy to be back in the U.S. again.

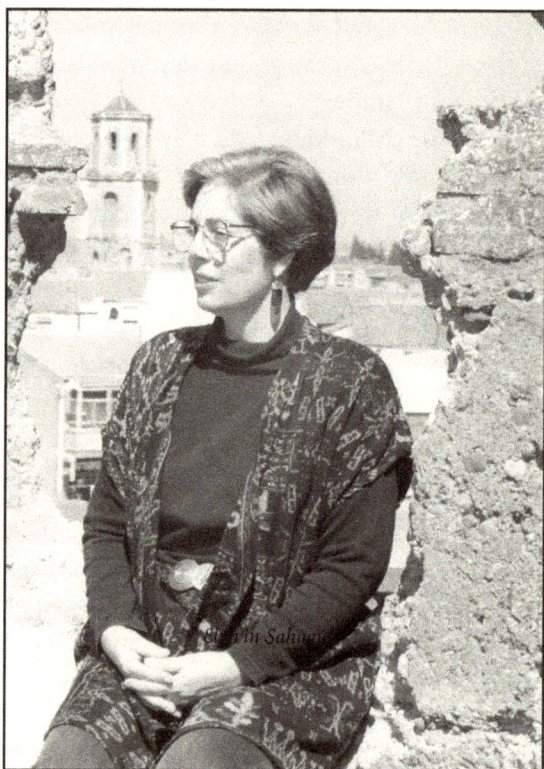

Elyn in Sahagún

Dating and Parking

When I was sixteen my world suddenly expanded. I was licensed to drive a car. Before that time, I was dependent on my parents or older friends to get to any place I couldn't walk. Now I could drive out into the country, or even to the next town, if my parents would loan me the car. At the same time, my relationship with girls changed drastically. I could date a girl and take her someplace we couldn't reach on foot, and I could be alone with a girl by driving her out in the country and parking on some deserted lane. In short, we were a part of those liberated generations of young people that came about with the advent of the automobile. We took full advantage of it.

Dating and "parking" were generally different activities and I did them with different girls. When I dated, I would ask a girl out several days in advance, and I was expected to pay for the entertainment and any refreshments. We would go to an event in some neighboring town, and I would bring her home and deliver her to her door, collecting a good night kiss as my reward. We were told that "nice girls don't kiss on the first date," but in my experience, most did. After all, we had all known each other from early childhood and had probably kissed on the school playground when we were in grade school.

"Parking" was a very different sort of activity. We boys would cruise around town in our cars and link up with girls who were walking on the streets or cruising in their own cars. The expressed intent in such cruising was understood to be picking up members of the opposite sex for purposes of parking. The girls understood this as well as the guys but would never admit it openly. My friend John and I were regular companions for many of these evening forays. We would see which of our parents would loan us the car and drop by and pick the other up to begin the hunt.

We were often successful and considered ourselves real "ladies men." In our junior year of high school we had some real triumphs. We were able to get a pair of senior girls to park with us sometimes. These two girls always traveled together, and we would leave one of our cars on the main street and go together to one of the many "parking places" we all knew about.

I should explain about our various parking activities: they had names and were considered to be in a progressive order. We spoke of getting to first base, second base, or hitting a home run. There was kissing, which was always the first activity. If kissing became deep and passionate, it was called necking. Passionate kissing was called French kissing because we believed those sensual foreigners must have invented it. The next level of activity (second base) was called petting, which came in two levels: light and heavy. Light petting consisted of feeling a girl's breasts and thighs through her clothing, while heavy petting involved getting under the clothing to the real thing. We seldom actually removed any of our clothing during heavy petting, but hooks, snaps, buttons, and zippers would be opened and clothing loosened to allow access. Petting to orgasm was considered to be "going all the way," as was actual intercourse. As a popular song of the time slyly stated, "When somebody loves you, It's no good unless she loves you, ALL THE WAY!"

We were both attracted and scared to death of sexual intercourse. In those days before the pill, we had to rely on cheap condoms (purchased out of machines in the men's rest room of some service station) that we had probably been carrying in our wallets for months. We knew that better-quality birth control was available at the drug stores, but we also knew that the clerks wouldn't sell it to us.

The two senior girls, Maxine and Jane (names changed to protect the guilty), would go with John and me only if senior boys weren't available. Their aim in parking was heavy petting, and they must have had some secret signal system that warned them when one of the boys was nearing orgasm because they would suddenly get out of the car and walk some distance away for a few minutes. Those minutes seemed like hours to two boys, left at the peak of passion to stew in their own juices. When the girls returned, they would be cool as cucumbers, and they would trade partners so we wouldn't try to start again where we had left off. They always feigned outrage at our previous misbehavior, but they would go out with us again the next evening if older partners weren't available.

If they had driven us to the parking spot, the girl in the front seat would suddenly start the car when we had reached the "danger zone" again, and the evening of parking would be over. If John or I had driven, the girls would insist that they had to be home by a certain hour and had to leave "right now." There were no romantic feelings amongst us at all. I would as often start the evening with Maxine as Jane, and I would probably be with the other by the end the evening. It was pure sexual exploration, and I leave it for the reader to judge who might have been exploiting whom in those evenings of passion.

John and I actually preferred parking with younger girls. They might not be as easy to get to the level of heavy petting, but they were not as well organized as Maxine and Jane. With other girls there was the thrill of the unknown and of pushing the limits of a less experienced girl; with Maxine and Jane we quickly learned what the order of business would be, and it never varied.

Parking with other girls was a bit "catch as catch can." The girls would be out in pairs, as singles, and in larger groups. It was often hard to negotiate getting two girls in our car at the same time, and on more than one occasion John or I would be taken home early so the other could park with the one girl we had been able to catch. This was the advantage of being the driver. The rider in the back seat had other advantages if we could find two girls. The back seat occupants could, of course, get a head start while the driver looked for an unoccupied parking place.

The cruising scene was not always limited to high-school kids. I well remember the fall of my senior year, when a new English teacher, fresh out of college, came to town. We were told later that she had had a strict religious upbringing and had gone to a fundamentalist

Christian college with severe restrictions on her behavior. She had never experienced anything like the nighttime scene I have described above, and she was drawn into it like a moth to flame. I parked with her several times, as did at least one of my friends. She was fired by the board of education early in the semester and had to leave town, her teaching career ruined. I have always felt some guilt at having been a part of her downfall, but if it hadn't been me, it would have been another boy.

Another "older woman" that cruised at night was the young wife of a local man. It seems that she had had complications after the birth of their child, and had had a hysterectomy. The freedom this gave her in the sexual area must have overwhelmed her (or perhaps something else was going on), and she "went wild." She would cruise the streets alone, and if you wanted to park with her, you would begin to follow her car. She would lead you to the city park, where you were to stop your car and turn off the lights. In a few minutes, if the coast was clear, she would return and pick you up. I was told that parking with her was never more than a twenty-minute affair. Her intent was to have intercourse as quickly as possible and return home before her husband suspected.

I was tempted to go with her, and on at least one occasion followed her to the city park, but I never stopped the car and waited to be picked up. As desirable as an easy lay with an "older woman" would have been, I simply couldn't be a part of such a sordid business. Her husband was one of my father's friends, and I had heard him talk about her poor husband, who was stuck home babysitting while his "slut of a wife was out looking for men." Little did he know that some of the "men" she found were my classmates. I now realize that this "older woman" was only three or four years older than me, and she was not more than a year or two beyond the high school cruising scene herself.

Of course, not all the boys and girls of the town were participating in the night-time scene. Some kids were more under their parents' thumbs and others were constrained by moral considerations. I would guess that the percentage of participants might be as much as 30% of the high-school age kids in town—and it wasn't just the "bad" kids who were out there. The daughter of one of the local fundamentalist ministers was often cruising with us and some of us were considered to be among the "good" kids in town.

All this nightlife seemed quite "wild" and exciting to us. Now I realize that it was just a game, with rules as strict as those of any sport. Our slang expressions: "getting to first base," "scoring," and "hitting a home run" were much more apt than any of us realized at the time. Parking was, simply, the only coeducational sport played at Cedar Vale High School, and a valid Kansas driver's license was your ticket of eligibility.

Raising Kids

I have been reluctant to write much about my two children, Stephanie and Greg, or my ex-wife out of respect for their privacy. However, there are many stories of my children's growing up that I have told many times.

My two children are as different from each other as any two people I could imagine. They arrived on this planet with their personalities well formed, and their growth and development just clarified and amplified who they already were. I gave them as similar upbringing as possible, given their different genders and the eighteen-month difference in their ages, so I can take very little credit for their adult personalities. I did the very best I could for each of them, giving them love and attention and supporting their education as best I could. I value each of them for how they have turned out to be. I think of them now as friends that I enjoy being with.

To give you a picture of these two wonderful human beings I will begin by describing their entries into the world. Steph arrived fighting. When breast feeding, she would arch her back and come down on the nipple with full force, as if she had to capture a fleeing animal. Greg, on the other hand, was quiet, patient, and easy going. He seemed to assume that everything would come to him with little effort, and it generally did.

Steph was absolutely fearless. One of her favorite activities as a baby was arching backward in my arms and diving head first toward the floor, depending on me to catch her ankles. I never missed, but there were some hair-raising moments. She would laugh uproariously every time she did her acrobatic trick. Greg, on the other hand, never went in for such daredevil antics, but in later years he took up rock climbing—without benefit of ropes and climbing gear.

Steph's voice was always several decibels louder than Greg's. I always knew the instant she arrived home by the sound of slamming doors and her exuberant greetings. Greg could be found in his room after school, in case I wondered if he was lost. I would not describe either child as introverted, but Greg was quiet and intensely interested in everything in the world. He was a scientist by inclination and preferred to spend his time examining details, while Steph got the general picture of how things were.

One day when Greg was about three I was driving him to an appointment. He was watching the road signs along the highway and said, "Dad, I'm going to learn to read." I responded, "How are you planning to do that, Greg?" "I'm going to look at every word very hard until I know it." It was only a few months before Greg could read his books to me. He seemed to have a disciplined, thoughtful approach to everything he did, and he generally accomplished what he set out to do. Steph, on the other hand, was given to wholehearted striving but would sometimes overshoot the mark. When she was ten or eleven, Steph became completely enamored with Wicca, an "earth-based" religion that was experiencing a renaissance at that time. She read everything she could find on the subject and declared that she was a witch. She was attending a summer camp for girls run by a local feminist group when I got a call from the camp director asking me to come and pick Stephanie up. It seems that she had been practicing witchcraft in the dorm room and had frightened the other girls, who reported her to their parents.

It was always apparent to me that we were raising two highly intelligent young people. Both possessed the ability to excel in academic pursuits. Their approach, however, was radically different. For example, Steph loved math and saw it as a puzzle-solving game. She would do every problem and ask her teacher for more. She solved the problems easily and enjoyed the "game." Greg, on the other hand, would do only enough to understand the concept and saw no reason to do more.

When he was a senior in high school I was called in by his calculus teacher. He told me that Greg had just scored above the 99th percentile on the math section of the SAT tests while, at the same time, he was earning a C in calculus. Greg simply would not do all the problems that were assigned once he understood the concept. I had to explain to him that a C grade would not serve him well when he applied to the top engineering schools in the country. He brought his grade up, was accepted at Carnegie Melon University in electrical engineering, and is having a brilliant career.

I always knew what was going on with Steph because she told me. Greg, on the other hand, was quite difficult to read. He would answer any question posed directly to him but volunteered very little to me. During Steph's high school years, I made it a practice to take a walk with her nearly every day. During that walk she would talk nonstop, telling me everything that was happening and how she felt about it. Sometimes I heard more than I felt comfortable hearing, but I always knew exactly what was going on. When I wanted to know about Greg's life I would have to think up a question that would give me an insight into his world. His answers were seldom more than one sentence in length. It was not so much that he was secretive, he just saw no reason to tell me every little detail.

There was, however, at least one occasion when Greg purposefully mislead me. I only learned about that a few years ago. One day, when he was a beginning driver, he and a friend asked two girls in an adjacent town for a double date to a movie. Greg called me to say that the car was out in the middle of a corn field along the highway between the two towns. "How did it get there, Greg?" I asked. "Well, there was a dog in the middle of the road and I swerved to miss it." I went out in the country and managed to get the car back on the road. There was minimal damage to either the field or the vehicle. A few years ago we were visiting Greg and Kristin's (Greg's wife) home and talking with one of their high school classmates, who was visiting them. Somehow the subject of the car accident came up and both men, try as they would, couldn't keep straight faces. They erupted in explosive laughter. Sensing that there was more to the story than I knew I pried into the incident. Greg admitted that he and his friend were just fooling around on the road and that there had never been a dog. "Well, I guess it is too late for me to ground you after all these years," I replied. How many other stories I know only part of, I can only guess.

One story I have told over the years to illustrate the unique qualities of my two children is, I admit, a complete exaggeration. I have often said, "Neither of my children will invite their friends over to our house—Steph because she is ashamed of how affluent we are, and Greg because he is ashamed of how poor we are." This story is untrue. Our house was generally filled with their friends. However, it does encapsulate a difference between them. Greg always wanted the best in everything he had. His room was plastered with photos of Lamborghinis and Porsches, and he has opted for a lifestyle that reflects his taste for quality. He is, however, very good with money and is not given to overspending his means. Steph was a counter-culture girl from the beginning. Material possessions never were important to her. She took in stray cats and would give anything away to anyone who might need it. Affluence was never her goal and she has achieved a lifestyle that is comfortable to her—one that is filled with cats, turtles, snakes, hamsters, and other creatures who need a home.

In many ways I see that my children have inherited parts of my personality. I was a "part-time hippie" who embraced the counter culture while maintaining a budding professional career that led to the academic and material success. Perhaps my children saw aspects of my personality that appealed to their fundamental inclinations and emulated them. In any case, I am happy with the way my children have grown into adults, and I like and respect who they have become.

Going to Sunday School for the First Time

April 8, 1945, Sunday Morning

Turning the corner by the post office I look down Main Street. There is not another soul in sight. On weekdays Main Street has a lot of activity, with people walking up and down, going in and out of stores, with knots of men on the corner talking and pairs of women standing in front of the stores, looking at the displays and talking with each other. Kids thread their way through the bustle, a smaller society that passes largely unnoticed below the adults. Like a bunch of mosquitos, we are ignored until we run into an adult or make too much noise. Now, on Sunday morning, downtown is deserted, like a ghost town. It's eerie being alone on Main Street—unsettling, but somehow comfortable too. I could go anywhere on Main street and not be noticed. I would have the whole town to myself.

Instead, I start up the hill toward the Methodist church, past the empty benches in front of City Hall. There are no old men out this morning, leaning on their canes and talking quietly with each other. As I get nearer to the church I'm filled with uncertainty and walk slower and slower. What will it be like there? Dad says that all that churches are good for is for people to squabble among themselves. Granddad says that he told the preacher he would only go to church if he would preach about man's duty to man rather than man's duty to God. He said the preacher told him he would be run out of town if he ever preached that sermon. So he says he never went. Granddad just laughed and laughed and slapped his knee when he said that. I didn't get the joke, but the message was clear enough. Mother is very silent when it comes to church, which is unusual for her.

Best be on my guard at the church until I get the lay of the land. I'll slip in and see what it's like. Maybe nobody will notice me at all if I'm real quiet. As I get near the church I begin to see cars driving up and parking. Families all dressed up, getting out of their cars, the kids heading into Sunday school. I see the kids going downstairs into the basement, so I slip down there, trying to be unnoticed. A few people say hello and tell me they are glad to see me there. I'm not sure why or if they really mean it. It may be that it's just the right thing to say on Sunday morning. The church basement with its cement floor painted with a shiny gray paint looks completely different from the times I was there before for some meeting or a banquet. No tables now—just rows of folding chairs all facing the front and lots of tan cloth curtains strung on wires overhead. I slip into the back and find myself a chair near the corner of the back row. Maybe I won't be noticed there.

After what seems like a long time the piano starts up—a jangling "honky-tonk"-sounding piano, and we are asked to turn to page 3 — "Onward Christian soldiers, Marching as to war, With the cross of Jesus going on before. . ." Visions surfaced in my mind of my uncle Vernon, in his army uniform, carrying a gun, shooting at Germans and Japs (that most hated enemy) and all the while a white cross floating in the air above him. Is that what the war is like, I wonder?

Women and kids singing and howling chorus after chorus, and the piano rattling away, and me feeling better, because one thing I love to do is sing, and some people say I'm good at it. This isn't so bad after all. They seem to get along with each other pretty well here. Now a prayer. Everyone with their heads bowed and eyes closed, and me peeking with one eye open a crack, to see what I ought to be doing, not really listening to the long-winded man using phrases like "We ask your blessing on," and "We ask that you to be with the poor and suffering." Finally he closes with "in Jesus' name, Amen. Now, please go to your classes." Where is my class? How will I know where to go? Everyone else seems to know. Some motherly older woman seems to sense my uncertainty and shows me the place—a little cubicle at the back of the church basement, made entirely of cloth curtains.

A group of kids from my class in school are already there. They are staring at me like I don't belong at all, and a few say some things to me. Not friendly things. I just try to ignore them and pretend to be real busy studying the flannel board at the front of the class. The teacher hands out "the lesson." It's a smallish piece of paper with a color picture of grown men wearing sheets and nearly barefoot on one side and a story printed on the other side. I've never seen a grown-up dressed that way and it's a mystery to me. We read the story together and the teacher does something with paper cutouts of people and animals and rocks that she moves around on the flannel board. I don't understand most of what she is saying, but at least nobody is staring at me anymore.

Then its time to memorize the bible verse. We repeat it over and over and then each kid has to say it without looking at the lesson sheet. That's easy enough, but I don't like everyone's eyes on me when it's my turn. Now it's time to see how many verses we can say from previous weeks. I'm in trouble now because there haven't been any previous weeks for me, and I am thankful that I'm in the back row. Maybe I can make myself nearly invisible by sitting low in my chair and hiding behind the head of the kid in front of me. The tension builds something awful as the teacher works her way down each row starting at the front. Some of the girls seem to be able to say a lot of verses, which they are very proud of, and some of the boys don't seem to remember very much, and their friends tease them by laughing and making faces.

Mercifully, the teacher passes right over me and I'm saved that terrible moment of embarrassment. I am really invisible now. It's like I'm not there, but that's better than being caught in the center of everyone's attention.

Now I become aware that I have to pee really bad, and I wonder how long this will go on, and can I make it home. I wouldn't move from my chair if my bladder burst, and I concentrate on holding out till this is over. I wouldn't want to have to ask someone here to show me the bathroom. They probably would just laugh at me for having to go to the bathroom at church. The rest of the class is just a blur as my attention is riveted more and more on internal matters. When the class finally winds down I feel like I am going to make it—but no, Sunday school isn't over yet. We all have to go back to the main room for "closing exercises." More hymns and people talking and the pressure building all the time. Finally the meeting breaks up and I hurry out as fast as I can while remaining invisible. If I ran someone might notice me. All the way home I can't think of the empty Main Street or the cars from church driving by. Everything is concentrated on the safety of the bathroom at home. When I make it without an accident I breathe a deep sigh of relief.

Later Mom asks me how it was and I say "OK." "Will you go back again?" "Maybe." There are a lot of mysteries there. Jesus, and Christian soldiers, and cutouts of people dressed in sheets being moved around on a flannel board. Bible verses to be memorized, and people singing and praying. I can't put it all together, and no one explains it to me, but everyone there seems to understand, and they think it is serious business, judging from their reverent tones and dress-clothes. Sure I'll go back. I'll keep slipping in and being invisible till I can get it figured out. Then maybe, some day, I'll be a part of something, and I won't be always alone.

Days of Reckoning

One morning in the early 1990s I awoke from a bad dream. Unlike most bad dreams, this one seemed to persist and follow me around like the little dark cloud that hung over the head of Joe Btfsplk in the Lil' Abner comic strip of our youth. There was simply no reason for the funk I was in. After all, my life was nearly perfect. I was at, or just past, the peak of my career. I had a good reputation as a composer and, in recent years, I had become known as a successful textbook author. The university had rewarded my long service in teaching, administration, and creative work with the highest rank they could bestow, distinguished professor. This got me a few hundred dollars additional salary and a parking spot right outside the music building. It also got me the honor of serving on the committee that chose a new university president and on other prestigious committees such as "promotion and tenure" and the like. My first wife and I had raised two wonderful children and had seen them through their university education and out on their own. The future was all smooth sailing.

Of course, I did average one migraine headache per week, but a combination of prescription drugs and regular massage kept that in check. The periodic diverticulitis could be handled with a round of antibiotics every month or so. My asthma was totally controlled with an inhaler, and my chronic acid reflux was nearly under control with the new drugs that were coming on the market. My enlarged prostate could be kept in check by herbs alone, so it was no problem. I was working an average of sixteen hours per day, seven days a week—and having fun doing it. There was simply no reason that the dream that

I was standing in front of my own grave, already dug, wouldn't go away.

I thought about that dream for several months and a series of questions arose in my mind. I began to wonder why I was working all the time I wasn't sleeping. I couldn't remember when I had last done something frivolous like going to a movie. I reflected on my list of stress-related illnesses. I no sooner would get one under control when another would come to take its place. I sensed that something was seriously wrong and I had to get to the bottom of it. Fairly soon I came to the conclusion that the reason for all the work was that I couldn't stand my home life. Our marriage had never been a close one, but we had done a good job with our children and there weren't any major wars going on between us. My wife was a respected attorney in town with her own very busy career. We enjoyed the good reputation that two successful people earn and we didn't lack for friends and acquaintances.

After an argument that was about something totally insignificant, I told her that I thought I was going to leave for awhile, and in an act that shocked everyone around, I moved out of the house. The next few months are just a blur to me. A friend, Ivy, had a room in her basement, behind her furnace. There was a full bathroom down there so when she invited me, I moved in. My bed was an old futon that was brick hard. My closet was nails driven into the walls around the room. I had one table and a chair. I was totally lost and Ivy was my port in the storm. I was still teaching full time, but I hardly remembered what I had taught ten minutes after the class. Twenty-eight years of university teaching gives one a certain backlog of lectures, and you can continue without much thought. I had bragged that someone could fire a starting pistol and I could deliver a 50-minute lecture without any preparation or even looking at my watch. I had some creative projects that were unfinished, but I could do them in the same way. I undertook no new projects however, and gradually my days began to open up.

I started a men's group where a group of guys could share their difficulties and challenges. Two of these guys were young people with small children. I began to hang around their houses and play with the kids. I joked that Indigo, the three-year-old daughter of one of the guys, was the best therapist I had. She loved to bonk noses, and I could bonk noses with Indigo for a few minutes and be totally relaxed. Most of the guys in the men's group were not university types, and I came in contact with a different part of society where the driven lifestyle of the professors I knew wasn't the norm. These people had time to be with their kids and time to read a novel or even go to a movie if I would babysit for them. I did a lot of free baby-sitting during those months, and my friends and their wives provided a lot of home cooked meals.

Gradually the fog began to clear and I moved into a small duplex apartment. At least I was above ground level. I enjoyed visiting with my new friends and the neighbors around me. The university had an early retirement program that provided very attractive options for professors, starting at age fifty-seven. I would be fifty-seven in 1994 and I began to make plans for early retirement. After about a year of fruitless marriage counseling, I filed for divorce. I was not prepared for getting a divorce from one of the top divorce attorneys in town. The divorce was fairly quickly granted, but the financial settlement took several years and ended up being argued before the state supreme court.

During the months of limbo I had wanted to keep my evenings busy. Going home to a dark basement room was just too depressing. The local Unitarian Fellowship had a very good program of adult education and I began to fill several evenings each week with classes. I liked the people I met there and one person in particular became a good friend. Elyn was in charge of adult education classes for the fellowship and had plans to go to seminary the following year. Her son was the same age as my son and was in the process of completing his college education. We had a lot in common, not the least of which was that her parents had been colleagues of mine at the university. Her father was also a distinguished professor, and Elyn had a Ph.D. in cultural anthropology. She was in a lot of the classes I was attending, including a Friday evening *satsang* (an evening of chanting and ceremony) for Mata Amritanandnamayi, a living Hindu saint. After a while, I asked Elyn if she would like to car pool to the *satsang*. After I filed for divorce, my friendship with Elyn took a new direction, and we became an "item." When she went off to seminary the following year I began to visit her in Denver as many weekends as I could.

By that time I was in my final year at the university, having declared myself in transition to early retirement. Elyn and I were married the following summer. I can truly say that my life has begun anew in the years that Elyn and I have been married. We have traveled, enjoyed our home life, and taken time to do fun things. Just tonight we attended a concert and, on the way home, we enjoyed looking at the full autumn moon, the brightest of the year because of the proximity of the moon to the earth. In my previous life I would scarcely have noticed. I have noticed that the shortening of daylight has begun to turn our plantings into their fall beauty and I will enjoy that transition. Life is good!

Since I have retired I have continued to come to grips with a lifetime addiction to work. Work addiction is unlike any other addiction —but instead of landing you in jail it is rewarded. Society loves a work addict. The more you can accomplish the better you are rewarded, and I had followed that carrot almost into the grave. I can't say that I have beaten this addiction. I am up at 1:00 a.m. writing this and I still put out a pretty full day of work most days. But at least I know the dimensions of the problem and make every effort to take my time, have some fun, and just spend time doing nothing. Doing nothing is not wasting time, it is taking the time to enjoy the small things. The small things can be sweet.

How I Became an Author

(For Fun and Profit)

One day in the mid 1980s I was sitting in my office at Iowa State University when there was a knock at the door. Two women introduced themselves as editors for Wm. C. Brown (a publisher of college level textbooks). College professors are often approached by representatives of textbook publishers who want them to adopt their books for their classes. I assumed this was just another sales call and invited them in. To get rid of a textbook salesman is relatively easy. You ask what new books they have to offer and select two or three to have them send sample copies. That generally satisfies them and they go on their way. In due course you get the books, spend a few minutes looking at them, and either put them on your bookshelf or toss them in the trash. (Unscrupulous professors get as many free books as possible and sell them on the used book market, creating a small profit center for themselves.) I started into my usual spiel, "What new books . . ." and the ladies stopped me cold. "We are not here to sell you books. We want to talk with you about becoming a textbook author."

It seems that they had a very successful two-volume textbook, *Music in Theory and Practice* (MTP) by Bruce Benward that they were having trouble with. Dr. Benward, it seemed, could not produce publishable manuscript without much editorial help. I was, of course, familiar with the history of this book. I had looked at the first edition with some interest because I agreed with its basic premise, that the beginning study of the theory of music should look at all aspects of music rather than simply concentrating on the study of harmony, as the traditional method had done. (I know you are all yawning by now, but these are the sorts of arguments that college professors engage in—rather like arguing about the number of angels that would fit on the head of a pin.) I had decided against adopting the first edition because it was filled with errors and seemed poorly organized. A second edition had been hastily put together a year or so later to try to correct the worst of the flaws, and that book had been relatively successful. To get a third edition out four years later, the publisher had hired a ghost writer to rewrite the manuscript. This version had been extremely successful and now they were looking for a long-term solution to their problem—how to get an author that they could depend on while keeping Dr. Benward's name on the book, which guaranteed sales. They had heard about me from another of their authors, who was on our faculty.

"Would you be interested in considering a joint authorship with Dr. Benward for *Music in Theory and Practice*?" I would have to say that such a thing was the farthest thing from my mind. At the time I was a very busy professor with a full load of teaching and a demanding career as a composer. The last thing I needed was another full-time career. However, I believe in never rejecting opportunities that appear on my doorstep without giving them some consideration (and this opportunity fit right in with my advanced case of workaholism). I agreed to go to the University of Wisconsin and meet with Dr. Benward for a discussion since the publisher was paying for the travel. My meeting with Benward was successful and we seemed to be a good fit for each other. I agreed privately with the publisher that I would be in charge of actually producing the future editions of the book and Benward would supply me with his ideas. That would work out well for everyone concerned, particularly in the financial area. Textbooks that are successful generate large sums of money, enough for everyone to be well paid for their efforts. At the time I didn't have need for additional income, since I was being paid well as a professor and my compositions generated a small income. As I looked forward to retirement, however, I thought I might need some additional income to supplement the largess of Social Security and my university pension.

I began work on the next edition of *MTP* and found that I actually enjoyed being an author. There was a lot to do to bring the book up to my standards. It needed to be reorganized and several new chapters written to fill gaps in the outline. Benward was easy to deal with, since all he appeared to want were the yearly royalty checks and the inclusion of a few of his pet ideas. He was happy to turn all the work over to me and collect his royalties. We produced the fourth edition of the book. It was even more successful than the previous editions.

With easy money coming in for the next four years (new editions are usually produced every four years), I began to think about other topics I might like to tackle as a sole author. The first of these was in the area of music fundamentals. I wanted to write a beginning textbook that wasn't the dry factual approach that music fundamentals had always been. (Music fundamentals, for all you non-musicians, is the study of music notation, scales, intervals, triads, key signatures, and rhythm—the fundamental building blocks of Western music.) I wanted to involve the student with making music as they learned these basic facts. The publisher bought my idea and I wrote *Music First!* (This book is now in its fifth edition and is also doing quite well in the textbook market.) When the manuscript for this book was finished I approached the publisher about doing the page layout for the book, a task that they normally contracted out. With my computer skills and the new page-layout programs that were coming on the market, I thought I could do the job and not have anyone else making mistakes and messing up my manuscript. I got the contract for this job, thus beginning what was to become yet another full-time job.

Never one to leave well enough alone, I authored and coauthored three more textbooks over the next few years and did the layout for all but the last one. The publisher was happy with my work as a "pager" for books and began contracting me for production of other textbooks they were bringing out. I accepted nearly all of these jobs. At one time, I was employing as many as ten student assistants to do research and to produce the short excerpts of music that dot music textbooks. I continued to do all the layout work. I was having fun and was working nearly all my waking hours, without regard for my health or the needs of those around me. With all the textbook work my career as a composer was being neglected. I'm sure that the quality of my teaching was beginning to suffer as well. If this sounds totally insane to you, well, it does to me too. Nevertheless that was how I chose to live about ten years of my life.

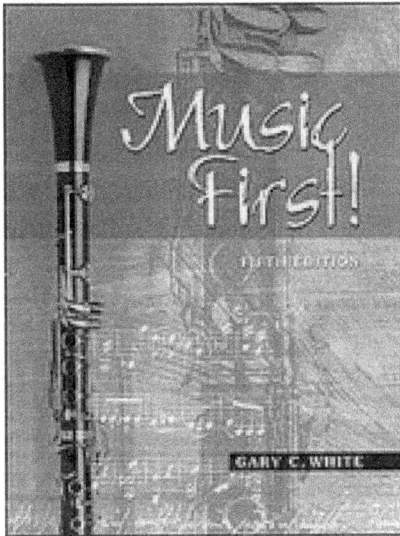

The Whitney Drug Store

The Whitney Drug Store was the setting for many of my memories of growing up in Cedar Vale, Kansas. As a youngster I was fond of visiting Mrs. Walker, the owner of the store. I would find Mrs. Walker sitting at the soda fountain in the evening. At night, customers would be few and far between, and I would sit with her and listen to her stories. Mrs. Walker had a wry sense of humor that always delighted me. I remember her description of the origin of humor as one caveman pitching a rock on the head of another caveman and laughing uproariously. She understood that aggression is often the basis of humor. (Elyn's late father, Leonard Feinberg, an expert on humor and satire, would have agreed.)

When I was around ten years of age, I would make a round of downtown Cedar Vale several evenings each week. I would first visit Bill Leonard at the movie theater for a talk and then walk up to spend some time with Mrs. Walker. She always seemed to have time for me. Mrs. Walker had a keen interest in my budding fascination with chemistry. Her contributions to that interest were an outdated copy of the *Merck Index* that she gave me and the fact that she would sell me any chemical in the pharmacy except hydrofluoric acid, which even she realized was much too dangerous for a 10-year-old boy to be fooling around with. She did sell me hydrochloric acid and sulfuric acid, and my fingers were often stained yellow with acid burns. Using the chemicals she sold me, I experimented with making gunpowder and gun cotton, along with many other foul-smelling mixtures. That I survived all my early chemical experiments is a wonder. (Sadly, such youthful chemistry experiments are now curtailed by stringent federal restrictions on chemical sales.)

The Whitney Drug Store pharmacy was what would now be called a "compounding pharmacy." Then it was just what Mrs. Walker did. Mrs. Walker was the local and only purveyor of many over-the-counter concoctions that had been invented by her father, the late Dr. Whitney. I well remember her back in the pharmacy brewing up another batch of Dr. Whitney's version of Pepto-Bismol™. It had a similar color and texture to the patent medicine product but included additional secret ingredients known only to her. I am told by another former Whitney Drug Store employee that Mrs. Walker had a special preparation to keep girls in top form during those "special times of the month." The mixture was described as black and horrible tasting, and the ingredients, of course, were secret, but it apparently allowed the girls to keep on working at full efficiency during their periods.

Many Cedar Valeians swore by Dr. Whitney's preparations. I wonder if the secret formulas died with Mrs. Walker or if her son, Dr. Bill Walker, one of the local physicians, kept them. Her preparations were not limited to remedies for her human customers. She also stocked a complete line of veterinary products that were in good demand among the farmers and ranchers in the Chautauqua County area.

The other drug store in Cedar Vale was much more like a modern pharmacy. Don Hankins only sold preparations that were marketed nationally, and his drug store was much more "upscale" than Mrs. Walker's establishment (see "Bill Leonard [1881-1952]" p. 7). I wonder who actually purchased prescriptions at the Hankins Drug Store, since Dr. Hays, the only doctor in town other than Dr. Bill Walker, maintained his own pharmacy and dispensed directly to his patients. Dr. Walker probably steered his patients toward his mother's establishment, so Hankins' clientele must have been what was left over, the patients of doctors in neighboring towns.

Mrs. Walker's daughter Julia ran a hair salon at the rear of the drug store. She was an avid amateur artist and she taught many of the children in town to paint in oils. I was one of her students. I remember spending many days in the corner of her shop painting amidst all the hair cutting, coloring, and "perming" that were going on all around. Julia would take a minute to look at what I was painting and make suggestions for improvements or techniques I might try. She never took one penny for her teaching, and she made a significant contribution to the artistic sensibilities of her students. I entered many of my oil paintings of landscapes and animals in the county fair in Sedan and was proud to display the blue and red ribbons I won. I also did oil paintings to give as Christmas gifts to my grandparents and other relatives.

When I was thirteen I applied for a job at the Whitney Drug Store and spent several years as a "soda jerk" and general clerk in the store. Mrs. Walker was not one to allow slacking. If there were no customers she always had a job for me to do, such as cleaning up, dusting the shelves, etc. I was paid $.25 per hour for my work. I thoroughly enjoyed the interactions with customers and making shakes, malts, sodas, cherry phosphates, and sundaes for the other kids in town. Mrs. Walker kept a stern eye on the quantities I used in my soda-fountain preparations lest I be too generous with the ice cream and chocolate syrup I used in the fountain preparations for friends.

Each year when Independence Day approached, a display counter near the front of the store was cleared out and restocked with all kinds of fireworks. Kids could place an order and have their fireworks put aside for them in brown paper sacks for later sale when their parents showed up. Firecrackers, big and small; skyrockets of various sizes and colors; sparklers; Vesuvius Fountains; whirligigs; and even those stinky black snakes that marred the sidewalks all over town—all were for sale at Whitney Drug. Every year one heard of fingers being blown off and eyes being put out, but it was all in the name of patriotic fervor and it was all legal. Cedar Vale didn't have a municipal fireworks display, so we made do with what we could purchase at Whitney Drug Store. I spent at least a week or two of my salary at the store buying fireworks each year. Mrs. Walker didn't offer an employee discount.

Speaking of salary, my payday was at the end of business on Saturday night. Saturday night was the biggest event in the commercial life of Cedar Vale, and the Whitney Drug Store was always packed all evening on Saturday. Mrs. Walker would pay me my wages as I was cleaning up at the end of Saturday evening. I had to be very careful because she would often try to short me on my pay. When I called her on it, she would grumble a little and cough up the rest of what I was owed. Mrs. Walker was not one to let our friendship or my young age get in the way of trying to maximize profits.

As I grew older I was offered a position as a clerk in L. C. Adam Mercantile Company, and I moved across the street to cleaner and better paying employment. I remember my years hanging around the drug store and working for Mrs. Walker with great fondness. I can say that Mrs. Walker was a significant practical teacher for me as I was growing up in Cedar Vale. I can still hear her cackling laugh at the absurdity of us humans and our foibles. Much of my present sense of humor was honed in her presence, and she also supported my early interest in science.

SCHOOL DAYS 1951-52
CEDAR VALE

Me at age 14.

Stella Beatrix Whitney/ Walker (1881-1962)

Describing the life of Stella Walker, proprietor of the Whitney Drug Store, and one of my early friends in Cedar Vale, Kansas, will entail several twists, turns, and detours to encompass a life that covered a wide range of both residences and pursuits.

Stella Beatrix Whitney was born in 1881, the second daughter of Dr. Perry N. Whitney. The earliest record I have found for P. N. Whitney is the 1880 Federal Census. In 1880 Perry Whitney (1865-?) was living in Union Center, Kansas, with his wife, Mamie (1856-1926), and infant daughter, Ethel. He listed himself as a farmer on that census form. By the 1885 Kansas Census the family had expanded to include Stella, age 4, and Francis, age 2. Perry was still listed as a farmer.

Sometime in the next ten years, Perry, Mamie, and family moved to Cincinnati, Ohio, where Perry attended the Eclectic Medical Institute and graduated with an M.D. "Eclectic Medicine" was a branch of medicine that enjoyed considerable popularity in the mid-nineteenth century. While it is now listed among the so-called "Quack Medicines" by the Food and Drug Administration and the American Medical Association, Eclecticism vied in the nineteenth century with allopathy, homeopathy, and other lesser-known philosophies, such as hydropathy, phlebotomy, and spiritualism. Eclectic physicians practiced a philosophy of "alignment with nature," learning from and us-

ing concepts from other schools of medical thought, along with obser-
vation of the use of medicinal plants by the Native Americans. There
was considerable controversy between allopaths, who believed in prescribing medicines to fight illness, and homeopaths, who believed in
prescribing minute amounts of the causes of the illness to boost the
immune system to fight the illness. Furthermore, allopaths were divided between the advocates for "botanical medicines" and advocates
of "mineral medicines." Mineral medicines became pharmaceutical
medicines, and botanical medicines became the province of herbal-
ists, naturopaths and the like. There is no need to tell you who won
that battle.

The Eclectics, who included Dr. Whitney, tried to remain above
the fray, preferring to pick and choose among all the methods of treatment. They often compounded their own medicines from combinations of "botanical" and "mineral" sources and created specific medicines for particular illnesses. The many preparations that Mrs. Walker
compounded from Dr. Whitney's recipes and sold over the counter at
Whitney Drug Store were typical "eclectic" medicines used by Eclectic
physicians.

By the 1895 Kansas Census, Dr. P. N. Whitney was living and
practicing in Cedar Vale, where he had moved after graduating from
the Eclectic Medical Institute. The 1901 history of Cedar Vale relates
that "for the past four years he has had the leading drug business in
the city. His daughter, Miss Ethel, is a very clever artist in oil painting; and another daughter, Miss Stella, who is studying pharmacy, is
very expert in crayon portrait work." Stella Whitney was in the very
first graduating class (1896) from Cedar Vale High School. The 1900
Federal Census lists the entire family (which now included another
daughter, Dorothea) living at home. Ethel was "at school" and Stella
(age 19) and Francis (age 17) were saleswomen at the Whitney Drug
Store. Sometime during the period, Stella attended the University of
Kansas, where she was one of the first women to graduate from the
pharmacy school.

Shortly afterwards, Stella met and married Reuben Gerald Walker
and the couple moved to Mounds, Oklahoma. The 1910 census shows
them living in Mounds, where Reuben lists himself as a "retail mer-

chant and druggist." Stella did not list an occupation during this period. Reuben had come from Highland, Kansas, where he had worked as a hired man on the Rolls Hunter farm.

Nothing is known of the couple for ten years. When we next meet them in the 1920 Federal Census, they are living in Dublin Gulch, Montana, where Reuben is employed as a miner. They have two children, Julia Irene (age 3) and William K (age 1), and Stella has no listed occupation. During this period Stella lost several babies, either early in life or before birth. The Cedar Vale Cemetery lists a plot with the designation "Infant children of Reuben & Stella [Walker] (no names, no dates).

In 1929 Stella moved back to Cedar Vale with her children, who now included Marcella (b. 1923) and Althea (b. 1925). There is no evidence that Reuben came back with them and there is no record of what happened to him after 1920. Stella is listed as the head of the household on the 1930 Federal Census. She was sharing responsibility with her sister, Ethel Whitney/Crabtree in running the Whitney Drug Store. Both women were registered pharmacists.

Stella's son, William, attended the University of Kansas, graduating with both a pharmacy and an M. D. degree in 1945. He then served in the U.S. Army until 1948, before returning to Cedar Vale to take up the practice of medicine. In 1955 he moved his practice to Sedan, approximately thirty miles east of Cedar Vale, where he remained until his retirement in 1988.

Ethel Crabtree died on October 25, 1951, and Stella became the sole proprietor of the Whitney Drug Store. I worked there around that time, but I don't remember Ethel taking part in the operation of the business. Stella Walker continued to run the Whitney Drug Store until her retirement in the late 1950s. She then moved to Sedan to be with William and his family until her death on October 19, 1962. Her ashes are in the Columbarium of Epiphany Episcopal Church in Sedan. She was a pioneer in advocating cremation in Chautauqua County, Kansas.

Stella B. Walker was an important figure in medicine in Cedar Vale, Kansas. While she was thoroughly trained in modern pharmacy, she maintained the eclectic remedies that her father P. N. Whitney brought to the town. Townspeople depended on Dr. Whitney's medicines for many of their ailments, and they missed Whitney Drug Store when it closed.

The 1902 Cedar Vale Girls Basketball Team
(Stella Whitney circled on the third row.)

The Cedar Vale Girls Band
(Stella Whiney circled on the top row.)

L. C. Adam Mercantile Company

My favorite job as a young person growing up in Cedar Vale, Kansas, in the early 1950s was clerking in the men's clothing division of L. C. Adam Mercantile Company. To say that L. C. Adam was the center of the downtown area of Cedar Vale, Kansas, would be an understatement. To a great extent, L. C. Adam's *was* the business district of the town. Adam's was a department store along the lines of the gigantic discount stores of the present day, where everything could be purchased. In the two-story main store (the tallest building in downtown Cedar Vale), the women's clothing and dry goods departments were on the left and the men's clothing department was on the right. Behind the men's area was the shoe department, where men's, ladies, and children's shoes and cowboy boots were sold. An adjacent one-story building housed the hardware store and grocery division, and in the back, across the alley, was the L. C. Adam Grain and Feed Store. The L. C. Adam Hay Barns were on the south edge of town, and the L. C. Adam Funeral Home was on a side street in a large older house, which may have been L. C. Adam's mansion in earlier times. The main store building had a huge open staircase in the center of the building that ascended to the second floor, which was at least twenty feet above the level of the main store. This upper level had once been a furniture store, but the only remaining evidence of that time was the showroom for caskets at the front of the building. Furniture for the living had long since ceased to be a profitable business in Cedar Vale, Kansas.

The main store was just the sort of place you see in movies of early twentieth-century towns. There were no cash registers anywhere in the store. Instead, there was a central business office on a balcony overlooking the main building and the building housing the hardware store. This office was connected to every division by overhead wires. The clerks in the hardware and dry goods divisions placed their sales receipts and the customers' money in small wooden cups that we attached to miniature trolley cars that hung from the wires. Clerks would pull on a rope, and that sent the trolley cars swishing up to the business office. There the bookkeepers, wearing green eye shades that made them look like croupiers in a gambling establishment, made the customers' change and recorded the sales in large ledger books, using fountain pens. Fountain pens had by this time replaced the dip models, but inkwells in the desks gave clear evidence of earlier times. If you didn't pull the rope hard enough, the cup stopped short of the office and drifted back down, amid the clerks' laughter. But, if you pulled the rope too hard, the little trolley crashed into the bumpers up in the business office, and the bookkeepers were not amused. When the transaction had been recorded a receipt and any change was placed in the cup and sent back to the clerk on the main floor.

One of the joys of working at L. C. Adam's was my easy conversations with customers as I was showing them goods or measuring them for sizes. All was unhurried and congenial. Customers and clerks alike enjoyed the shopping experience. A lot of local news and even gossip were shared in these exchanges.

There was very little that you couldn't purchase at L. C. Adam Mercantile Company. I remember that I once wanted sealing wax to create fancy seals on some document I was creating for a grade school project. I wanted to have the kind of seal that had ribbons pressed under a puddle of wax, which was stamped with a "royal" insignia. A clerk in the hardware division took me down into the basement of the store, where row upon row of shelves held a bewildering array of merchandise, and sure enough, high on a shelf in that dark space he found a stock of sealing wax that had been there for an untold number of years.

The upstairs storage area, in what had been the furniture department, gave mute evidence of other former L. C. Adam's enterprises. There were advertising materials for farm implements, tractors, cream separators, and even automobiles, all of which had at one time or another been available from Adam's.

At the front of the men's clothing department was a large glass case that held the stock of men's hats. There were large, cowboy-style Stetson hats and also men's dress hats. Each dress hat came in an oval box that had a picture of a beaver on the lid. In front of the hat case was a glass-topped counter that held men's ties. Next to that were sample dress shirts, also in glass cases with the complete stock in boxes on the shelves behind. Dress clothing was always shown behind counters or in glass cases, and the customer had to ask to see the merchandise. Only work clothing was out on the floor in open shelves and cases where the prospective buyer could touch it.

When I was a high-school senior, L. C. Adam Mercantile finally went bust. The automobile, which made it all too easy to shop in nearby Arkansas City, was largely responsible, I suppose. Perhaps a more important factor was that the stores in the larger towns were more "up-to-date," and people began to look down on the store's old-fashioned ambiance. An outside sales company was brought in to sell everything in the store and the atmosphere I had enjoyed so much was completely destroyed. The front windows were plastered over with huge, hand-painted "going out of business sale" signs, and the outside people were all business. Primarily they wanted the clerks to move the merchandise, something that had never been stressed by the previous management of the store. There wasn't time to talk with the customers, and everything was put out where people could handle it, which made the job of the clerk only one of taking the money and writing the receipt. There were no quiet conversations while helping people make their decisions. It took over one month to clear out the store, and toward the end, a lot of cheap and shoddy merchandise was trucked in to keep the shelves filled. I was embarrassed to be a part of the enterprise and ashamed that the long tradition of excellence that L. C. Adam's had built should come to this tawdry end. Finally the sales company moved on, and the huge store stood empty and gathering dust.

When I returned to Cedar Vale for my thirtieth high-school class reunion, I found the L. C. Adam Mercantile building had become the town museum. Now the old building was filled to the brim with memorabilia from all over the town and surrounding areas. It was an interesting museum, as small-town museums go, which isn't saying much. I couldn't help but think that the L. C. Adam Mercantile Company in its prime had better represented life in a small rural Kansas community in the early twentieth century than all the museum displays that had been so carefully prepared. In the museum they had installed Herb Marshall's counter from the hamburger joint around the corner (see "Dining Out in Cedar Vale, Kansas," p. 65). The equipment was all there, but not the greasy smell of the hamburgers and chili. There was also Herb Stone's dental chair, but not the dusty office I remembered (see "Dentistry in Cedar Vale," p. 86). Also gone were all those colorful characters that I remember with such fondness from when I was growing up in Cedar Vale.

My memories of Cedar Vale are a rich tapestry with many hues, both light and dark, while today's Cedar Vale reality is like a faded photograph that is recognizable, but a poor likeness.

The L. C. Adam Mercantile Company,
now the town museum.

The High School Auditorium

The building that housed Cedar Vale High School was both ingenious and dysfunctional in its construction. Built on a hillside with
the main entrance on the north (the upper level) and the auditorium
on the south (the lower level), one could approach the building on two
different levels. This allowed for two entrances to the main floor of the
auditorium on the south and two entrances to the auditorium balcony
through the main entrance on the north—very ingenious. However,
the problem with this arrangement was that the gymnasium was on
the floor above the north entrance and also above both the auditorium
and its balcony, making it impossible to schedule any serious activities
in both spaces simultaneously. The basketball fans had to negotiate a
flight or two of steps to ascend to the gymnasium above. In addition,
the gymnasium had large open windows on three sides looking into
the upstairs hall with the business, typing, study hall, library, English,
choir, and social studies classrooms on the other side of the hall. This
must have caused much gnashing of teeth and tearing of hair for the
school administration who needed to schedule both academic classes
and physical education classes at the same time. The noise from the
gym classes must have been very distracting, both in the auditorium
below and the classrooms surrounding the gym. The conflicts would
have been fairly manageable in the fall, when football was in season,
and in the spring, when track kept the athletes outdoors. But during
basketball season, which was a very important sport in Cedar Vale,
the scheduling must have been horrendous.

My first memory of the high-school auditorium was when the Cedar Vale grade school did a production of *Snow White and the Seven Dwarfs* and we got to use the big auditorium. I was eight years old and in the third grade at the time. We were all in elaborate costumes that our mothers had made. The production was at least as wonderful as the Walt Disney version we had all seen at the movies, or so it seemed to us. I was Grumpy, one of the seven dwarfs. Wayne Woodruff was Doc; Jack Foster was Dopey; Bob Cable was Sneezy; Marilyn Casebolt was Happy; Gloria Sanborn was Sleepy; and Jimmy Corder was Bashful. Don Shaffer, who was three years older, was the Prince, and Jo Ann Stone was Snow White. I remember that the production spilled over from the stage to the aisles and areas below the stage and there were elaborate sets throughout the auditorium. We had definitely made "the big time" in show business with that production and our parents were lavish in their praise.

My second memory of the auditorium was when, although I was only in seventh grade, I was promoted to a place in the high-school band (see "Mr. Beggs and the High School Band," p. 123). We rehearsed and did concerts there. Again, the auditorium spelled "the big time" for me, and I always maintained a certain respect for and awe of the place.

Once I got to high school the auditorium became the place for school assemblies, programs of traveling guest lectures, and the like. In particular, I remember a program given by a Native American man who was lecturing against the use of tobacco. As part of his presentation he took a section of auto inner tube and inflated it to bursting with his breath, thus showing the strength of breath a nonsmoker could achieve. I think he may have come on more than one occasion during our high-school years. I also recall those occasions when all the girls met in the auditorium and the boys met in the gym above for elementary sex education. There was an air of secrecy and intrigue about these meetings, with each sex not knowing what the other group was discussing.

The auditorium was also where we put on major cultural events and the aura of the arts hung about the place. The faint echoes of concerts, plays, and musicals reverberated in the air of the auditorium.

Mrs. Morris, our high-school vocal instructor, put on two major productions in the auditorium. The most elaborate was a production of Gilbert & Sullivan's *The Mikado*. The production was double cast and there were two performances, one with each cast. Mrs. Morris had meetings in her home for the cast, where she played recordings of the operetta and showed pictures of the costumes. The history of operetta in England was presented, and we were thoroughly indoctrinated about the importance of what we were about to do. Costumes were rented from a theatrical rental place in distant Kansas City. I well remember when the costumes arrived in trunks and we all tried them on. We had definitely arrived in "show business" with this production with its wonderful costumes and sets. Mrs. Morris was the one-person orchestra. She was an accomplished pianist, and the production was probably the best vocal production that was done by the students of CVHS, at least while I was a student there.

On another occasion Mrs. Morris put together a vaudeville-like review, with a script she wrote herself and songs drawn from the popular repertoire. This was a much lighter affair but it was great fun for all of us. Of course, the auditorium was also the scene for band and chorus concerts. There were special concerts by those students who were performing in the district and state music festivals.

As a special dispensation, I was allowed to go to the auditorium during my study hall periods to practice my trumpet. In my senior year, Mr. Barr, our new business and typing teacher, would sometimes join me there to accompany me on the piano. Mr. Barr was a gifted amateur pianist who played mostly by ear, made up his own songs, and enjoyed having me play them with him. He wore a hearing aid in one ear and was otherwise quite distinctive to me because he was a professed agnostic. I remember having serious religious discussions with him and feeling some pity that he was bound for hell. He seemed like a perfectly reasonable and caring human being—except for that fatal flaw. Somehow I never applied that same fate to my grandfather Call, who was also a rabid agnostic (see "Visiting Grandparents," p. 68).

In our junior and senior years we performed class plays in the auditorium. We all got together to build and paint a complete set using flats left over from previous productions. In particular, I remember our senior-class production of *Arsenic and Old Lace*. I had great fun playing Teddy and running about the stage blowing a bugle. The production was directed by Mrs. May Robinson, a prominent local citizen, due to the early departure of our young female English teacher (as described in "Dating and Parking, p. 15).

When I think about the range of shows we managed to produce with our tiny student body of not much more than one hundred and twenty students, I am amazed at how we did it all. The auditorium and our school productions were a cultural center of the town, and we were kept very busy and engaged much of the time. The town of Cedar Vale was blessed with much local talent, and we students made genuine contributions to the artistic quality of life there.

A Healing

A part of my ongoing spiritual practice for the past fifteen years has been going on individual silent retreats. In a typical individual silent retreat the retreatant is housed in an isolated cabin or in some other way placed where he or she will be unlikely to encounter other people. Provisions are made for food and other needs to be met in isolation. Retreats may be guided or unguided. I will describe a fourteen-day guided retreat I did at the Abode of the Message in the Berkshires in upstate New York. The Abode, which is the U.S. headquarters of the Sufi Order International, is located on the site of one of the original Shaker communities. Some of the buildings at the Abode date back to the late eighteenth and early nineteenth centuries.

I was housed in a tiny one-room cabin high on a hillside above the main buildings at the Abode. I was provided with a supply of food that I could prepare for breakfast and lunch. A hot dinner was brought to my cabin by the staff of the Abode and left outside the door. During the fourteen days I spoke only to the person who was guiding my retreat. My guide would visit each morning to check on me and to give me practices for the day. These interviews generally lasted for twenty minutes or so and consisted of my description of what had happened the previous day, some dialogue about my progress, and the assignment of the day's practices. My days were spent doing the practices, listening to music on my iPod, taking walks in the woods, sleeping, and occasionally reading material that was suggested by my guide.

It is impossible to convey what effect silent retreat has unless you have experienced it. There is a paring down and stripping away of external parts of the personality and a growing awareness of areas of one's personality that are generally hidden from view. One can swing between deep depression and crisis to near ecstatic states. I was about midway through this retreat when the following event occurred.

It was during the night-time hours. I was using only a single candle, having determined at the beginning of the retreat to go entirely on sun time and not use any form of electric light. I was in the dark, meditating, when a realization hit me suddenly and without warning. I realized at that instant that I had been afraid during my entire life. Along with this realization came an intense pain in the area in my lower abdomen where the prostate resides. I knew about where the prostate was because I had had a biopsy of the prostate several years earlier and had a history of prostate-related health issues. I also felt a constriction in the diaphragm region, all the way around my body.

The realization of my permanent state of fear was completely unnerving and after struggling with panic for an hour or so, I took advantage of an offer my guide had made that if I needed help she was available day or night. Since it was the middle of the night and I wouldn't encounter anyone, I walked down to the main buildings and called my guide from the public phone there. We talked for about an hour and she suggested practices for me to do that had the effect of relieving my panic enough so that I could sleep.

In the morning I examined my life in greater detail to see how this permanent state of fear had come about and why I had not been aware of it before. I looked at the time period when I was growing up and saw the fear of World War II that was constantly in the background (see "World War II Memories," p. 61). I looked at my mother's constant state of fear (see "Swimming," p. 165). I realized that my father lived in fear of my mother. I remembered again the constant fear I felt on the grade school playground (see "Bullies," p. 125). Wherever I looked I saw a pattern of fear that I had lived with until it became totally unconscious. I was like a fish in water, unaware of what I lived and breathed.

Bringing this fear to consciousness, I could see that there were more or less permanent constrictions in my body in the diaphragm area and perineum (the prostate region) that had had an effect on my health. I had suffered from asthma and other allergic responses in my lungs for most of my life. I saw that my chronic acid reflux disease might be related to constriction of the esophagus as it passed through the diaphragm. For many years I had had periodic difficulty with swallowing, sometimes leading to food being caught in the esophagus just above the diaphragm area. And finally, I had had a condition called benign prostatic hyperplasia (BPH). Before starting the retreat, an MRI of my prostate had revealed a lump that the doctor wanted to biopsy when I returned home.

My guide suggested a series of practices to address this state of fear. After several days I noticed that the pain in the prostate had gone away. Somehow I knew that the condition was going away and that I would be all right. Other symptoms began to show improvement as well, all due to my bringing my underlying state of fear to consciousness and working directly with it by doing practices.

When the retreat was over I returned home and went immediately to my urologist for a checkup. She was totally amazed to find that the lump had completely gone away and that my PSA (Prostate Specific Antigen) levels had lowered significantly. She told me that if she had not had her original diagnosis confirmed with an MRI she would have been sure that she had made a mistake in her original examination. She wanted to know what I had done in the month since the original examination, so I told her about the experience during the silent retreat. While she didn't deny that the retreat experience may have had some effect, I think she just thought of this minor miracle as one of the several unexplained events she had seen in her many years of medical practice.

All this took place several years ago and I continue to work with my underlying fear. I have noticed a marked decrease in my other symptoms, but the healing of my prostate stands out in my mind as the clearest evidence I have for the interrelationship of the body and the mind. Mystics say that the body is simply a covering that the soul takes on and grows while incarnated on this earth. If this is the case, a healing at the soul level can, indeed, make major changes in the body. Scientific medicine makes little or no place for healing at the soul level, but that may be the most important healing of all.

Winning Prizes

Elyn has suggested that to make the record of my life complete there needs to be an accounting of the prizes and awards I won during my forty-odd years of work as a composer. I must admit that at this point in my life I couldn't bring any of the details to mind, but through the magic of computers and the fact that I never throw any files away, I've reconstructed the following account.

The first serious prize I won was quite unexpected. A few years after I began teaching at Iowa State Univeristy I entered a composition called "Composition for Piano, Brass, and Percussion" in the Symposium for Contemporary Music for Brass at Georgia State University. When the piece was accepted I arranged to go to Atlanta for the performance. At the time I was romantically involved with a young woman who lived in the area and I arranged to meet her there. I planned to go to the performances as required, but my real reason for going was so that we would have a few evenings on the town in Atlanta. Imagine my surprise when the judges, who consisted of the members of the New York Brass Quintet, voted my piece the winner. The prize consisted of a cash award for writing a piece to be premiered by the NYBQ the following year at the 1975 Symposium. I was totally unprepared for this honor. There was, however, a hang-up. I was to be the guest of honor at a reception to be held in the evening after the Symposium was finished, but my woman friend and I had other plans. So I informed the people at the Symposium that I would not be able to attend their reception. You can imagine how that went over. Well, we had our evening in Atlanta and I went home to compose the work for the NYBQ.

The Quintet were all quite polite about the slight I had handed them in Atlanta. They gratefully accepted the piece I wrote and not only premiered it the following year in Atlanta but also put it into their repertoire for the next few years. However, when I went to Atlanta the following year for the premiere, there were those at Georgia State University who were just a bit icy in their welcome. I had learned a serious lesson with this escapade, and I never again mixed my personal life with my professional responsibilities as a composer. Looking back now, I can't believe I acted the way I did. However, it reveals a characteristic of mine, which is that when I make a plan I really like to stick to it.

The following year I entered a carillon piece called "Rotation" in a competition to be held in Holland at 's-Hertogenbosch. When the piece won the prize I had already made plans to be traveling in Europe. It was easy to include a quick trip to Holland for the performance and to accept the prize, which was a cash prize plus publication of the piece by Donamus, the largest music publisher in Holland. This time I made sure that my wife was with me and everything went beautifully. The Dutch really know how to make a presentation. The lord mayor of 's-Hertogenbosch made the presentation at the city hall, with several hundred people in attendance. There was a lavish reception, with a break during which cigars were handed out and smoked, another break for serving *genever,* a very powerful Dutch gin, all followed by the lord mayor in full costume, including a velvet hat and a very heavy silver necklace, delivering a half-hour speech, all in Dutch of course. Then a helpful soul gently pushed me forward to accept my prize. I must say that this was the most festive and wonderful presentation I attended until my retirement reception at Iowa State University.

Other prizes pale in comparison, although some were notable. There was the Composer's Competition Prize at Wabash College, a college for men in Crawfordsville, Indiana. The piece was "Chronovisions for Band," which I remember them slaughtering at the concert I attended to accept the prize. There was the Kendor Music/University of Maryland Clarinet Choir Composition Prize (try creating a shorter version of that name) for "Convolutions for Clarinet Choir." Then there was the Shenandoah/Percussion Plus Prize in 1982 for a piece called "Personae for Viola, Violoncello, and Percussion," which I can't for the life of me recall ever writing.

The two prizes that I most cherished were not prizes for a single composition but were awards for lifetime achievement. The women's fraternity in music, Sigma Alpha Iota makes an annual award to one musician in the U.S. and they gave me the title of National Arts Associate in 1985. In 1988 the University of California in Berkeley gave me the Berkeley Medal for my lifetime contribution to the literature of the carillon. While I don't consider having made a significant contribution to the carillon literature a big deal, the Berkeley Medal is about the equivalent of an honorary doctorate, which is a big deal.

All these prizes and awards are listed in the curriculum vita I found on my computer, and they certainly helped gain me the biggest prize of all, the rank of Distinguished Professor of Music at Iowa State University. That, as I have mentioned, got me a small raise in salary and a choice parking spot right next to the music building.

I was very proud of my accomplishments and they gave me publicity that brought increased possibilities for performances and commissions. My ego was certainly stroked by this recognition. The compositions themselves were competitive with others that were entered or they would not have won prizes. However, at this point in my life I am more intrigued about how I was negotiating my professional and private life and what my internal experiences were. Those experiences are much more interesting to me than the compositions I wrote and the prizes I won.

High-tech Communications

The telephone office was a communications hub for Cedar Vale, Kansas, and the surrounding rural communities. Located in a house on Highway 166 just south of the high school, the office was run by a woman named Molly Leniton, who was the chief operator. Molly lived in the part of the house that wasn't used for the telephone equipment. She had just two rooms at the back and the bathroom down the hall from the central telephone office. In the office were a pay phone booth, the switchboard, and all the electronics to operate the phone system, along with two desks where people could come in and subscribe for service or pay their bills. Molly hired several operators to help her run the switchboard, which had to be working twenty-four hours per day, seven days per week, with no closing for holidays. She hired my mother as an operator when I was about eight years old. We happened to be living across the street from the office, and I spent considerable time there when my mother was working evenings.

Cedar Vale had an old magneto telephone system dating from the early years of the twentieth century. All the lines came directly into the central office and were connected to the switchboard by an electronic mainframe on the back of the board. Power was supplied by a transformer on an adjoining rack, with banks of wet-cell batteries to provide backup in case of power failure. I remember that the batteries were clear glass and I could see the electrical components floating in acid within.

The switchboard had a jack (hole in the board) for each line in and out of the system, and a little trap door (called a "drop") above each jack. The drop would open up when the party on the other end cranked their phone. (Yes, you youngsters, phones had hand cranks on the sides of them in the early days. Later phones were equipped with an electronic device that sent a signal to the switchboard when the handset was picked up and another when the handset was replaced.) When a drop fell, the operator connected a plug to the jack and answered the call with the standard "number please" that was required of all Bell Telephone operators. Then the party would give the number and the operator would connect the call using the other half of the pair of plugs that were recessed into the base of the switchboard toward the back. If the number was busy, my mother would say "that number is busy" and remember to call the party back when the line was free. Her memory for such details was unerring and she would often be able to tell a caller that a party wasn't home but had called in from some other place in town and they might try to reach them at that number. As you can see, the telephone operator had a unique, and fairly complete, picture of what was going on in our little town.

When a caller completed a call they were supposed to "ring off" by turning the crank on their phone. Many people forgot that part of the process and the operators had to poll all active connections from time to time to see if people were still talking. That this led to overhearing parts of conversations and some outright eavesdropping goes without saying. My mother was not above listening in when business was slow. I well remember her coming home steaming mad at my father after one such overheard conversation. Of course, the callers would recognize the voice of the operator and might assume that my mother would be listening in, which in this particular instance she was. In a conversation between two ladies of doubtful reputation in the town, Mother heard one say to the other, "That Charlie White is a handsome man. He could put his shoes under my bed any day." Well, Mother arrived home with steam coming out of both ears and my father, who was totally innocent, didn't hear the last of it for months. Such were the "wages of sin" in Cedar Vale—in this case, the sin of listening in on other people's conversations.

The telephone switchboard was the best predictor of weather in the region, far beyond anything you could hear on the radio. When lightning struck anywhere in the western half of Chautauqua County drops on the switchboard for that area would all fall at the same time. Really big storms would result in all the drops falling at once, and the operator would have a full-time job replacing them. The job of operator was not without danger. Operators would report situations where balls of lightning fire came out of the face of the switchboard and dance around the office.

The "country lines" were party lines with two to six people on a single line. Many of the town lines were also shared in that way. The operator had to remember how many rings each party on a party line was assigned and ring their phones accordingly. People on party lines had to put up with constant eavesdropping from other people on the line. I remember a farmer, one of my dad's customers, who always answered his phone, "Good evening, friends and neighbors," which would be followed by clicks on the line as the guilty parties hung up their phones.

It is not an exaggeration to say that the telephone office was the hub of local communications. When the Cedar Vale system was replaced by dial phones, many people told my mother, who became the chief operator when Molly retired, that the new service just couldn't compare with the old hand-cranked system. People missed the personalized attention they were used to, even if it meant that others always knew all their business. When Mother became the chief operator the rooms where Molly had lived remained empty since we were a family of three and there wasn't enough room for all of us there.

World War II Memories

Much of my early life in Cedar Vale, Kansas, was colored in one way or another by the ongoing war. My first memory is a car ride I took with my father to deliver my uncle Vernon to Ft. Leavenworth before he was transferred to India to help build the China-Burma Highway. I don't think I could have been over three years old at the time, but I remember Dad and Vernon riding in the front of the car and me mostly sleeping in the back. I remember waking up when they got to Leavenworth in the middle of the night and I saw the men in uniform and guards standing at the gates. We said our good-byes. Dad must have driven home directly and without sleeping. It would be several years before we would see Vernon again, but grandmother had letters from him that had been photostated™ after parts had been blacked out. The whereabouts of service men, particularly those on sensitive missions, was withheld from their relatives.

My next memory of the war is seeing the black newspaper head-lines and the war photos that accompanied them. The adults gathered around their radios for news of the war every day and read Ernie Pyle's articles in the newspaper. Of course, the most graphic images of the war were those that passed by our eyes in the newsreels at the movies. My friends and I played war all the time, using the balsa-wood air-planes that came inside Kellogg cereal packages that we carefully cut out and assembled. I knew that very important things were happening in the world, but I had little sense of where these events were taking place. Many of my friends' fathers were in the service, and their moth-ers were left at home to raise the kids and try to make ends meet. My father never was drafted because his occupation (delivering gasoline to farmers) was deemed vital to the war effort. Mother was in constant turmoil thinking that he would lose his deferment at any time and we'd be left alone. She was already working for the telephone company and making a reasonable income, but she was always in fear for Dad's life should he be drafted.

Many items were rationed during the war. We had coupon books for many food items, and there was a lot of trading of coupons back and forth among the neighbors for items that each preferred or didn't need. A much more obvious impact for my family was that gasoline was also rationed. My father had to collect coupons for every gallon of gas he sold and had to account for them. I remember him sitting at home with small mountains of cardboard coupons, counting and counting to try to get the coupons to match the level of the tanks in his storage yard in the south part of town. It must have been a difficult task because he was always in a state of anxiety about it.

Another memory I have was the night that a train-load of German prisoners of war came through Cedar Vale. It was dark and many people, my family among them, turned out to see the enemy in the flesh. Each train car was lighted inside and was filled with young men in uniform. Soldiers with machine guns stood at each end of the car to keep the prisoners from escaping. I don't know what the young Germans would have done if they had managed to escape into the wilds of southern Kansas, but the U.S. Army took no chances. Or perhaps the soldiers were protecting the prisoners from irate U.S. citizens in the towns they passed through. When the train stopped at the railway station to take on water and coal, we were face to face with the enemy. Ugly cat-calls came from the crowd, and the Germans on board threw out paper water cups and other small pieces of paper with slogans such as, "Kill the Jews and the war is over." It was altogether an impressive sight, and it is burned into my memory in vivid detail. My father collected one of the cups, which had swastikas drawn all over it.

The cup became one of the mementos of the war at our house, along with some K rations (see "Firebug," p. 171), and a piece of paper with pigs printed all over it that became a picture of Hitler's face when folded in a certain way. We also had a few of uncle Vernon's photo-stated™ letters from India and some Indian money that he brought back from the war.

For children of that era, the war seemed to have always been with us and would always be there. My first indication that the world could change, and sometimes drastically, was the death of President Roosevelt. I was alone at home at the time and listening to the radio. Dad was delivering gasoline and Mother was across the street working at the switchboard. To me, Roosevelt had always been president and the news of his death came as a terrible shock (see "Milestones," p. 143). It was rather like hearing that God had suddenly died. I remember running across the street to deliver the news to Mother and wondering what might happen next.

What happened, of course, was President Truman and then the news of the bombing of Hiroshima and Nagasaki. Suddenly the war was over and we were launched into the Atomic Age. We had no idea what that meant. We were several years away from the "Duck and Cover" era, when school children were taught to duck under their desks in case of atomic attack. What an exercise in futility that would have been.

There was general rejoicing in Cedar Vale at the end of the war. The old jail that sat behind the City Hall was dragged out into the intersection next to L. C. Adam Mercantile (see "L. C. Adam Mercantile Company," p. 44), the post office, and the City Hall, and a huge nighttime bonfire consumed the jail building. Since I was living only a block away I was able to be there for the whole affair. I remember the flames that shot up higher than the top of the Adam's building amid the excitement of the gathered citizenry of Cedar Vale. That we made it through that escapade without burning down other buildings is a wonder.

I have often speculated about the meaning of the jail burning to Cedar Valeians. Did we think that there would be no crime after the war? Did the building simply need to be razed and this was a good excuse? A fellow Cedar Valeian tells me that it was simply the spontaneous work of several citizens who had a snoot full of booze at the time.

Perhaps they had spent a night or two in that little jail building and took the opportunity to vent their spleen. It was clearly not an event sponsored by the city fathers of the town, but the general euphoria of the end of the war must have precluded prosecution of the arsonists. In any event, it was not long before a new concrete-block jail went up on the same site and Cedar Vale again had a place for drunks to sleep it off. That little concrete-block building is still the city jail for the town.

My Uncle Vernon off to World War II.
His little dog "Pooch" also at attention.

Dining Out in Cedar Vale

There were limited possibilities for eating out when I was growing up in Cedar Vale, Kansas. This reflected the fact that most of us seldom, if ever, ate anywhere but home. I know my parents couldn't afford to do so very often.

By far the most popular eating establishment was Herb Marshall's hamburger joint on Highway 166, down the block from the bank building on the north side of the street. When there was something going on that brought rural folk to town, I would often see people out on the street waiting for a place at Herb's counter. "The joint," as everyone in Cedar Vale called it, could only accommodate ten or so patrons at a time. There was a long counter running the length of the place. Herb and his wife, Hazel, stood behind the counter frying hamburgers, dishing chili, and filling coffee cups. There were one or two small tables in the corners of the tiny building. That just left room for people to come in the front door and order hamburgers "to go." When I was growing up, Herb's hamburgers were always $.10 each. Inflation must not have been much of a factor in the 1940s and 50s. The hamburgers were hot and steamy and fried with the best-quality grease you could get anywhere around.

As good as the hamburgers were, Herb's chili was considered to be his real claim to fame. Hot, thick, and fragrant, Herb's chili was a treat we reserved for special occasions at the White household. The smell of the chili mixed with frying beef was like a magnet drawing the citizens of Cedar Vale down the street and into the joint. Later, when I had money of my own, I would sometimes indulge myself with a bowl of Herb's chili with beans. If I could go back in time I would certainly head for Herb's and have another meal in those wonderful, grease-soaked surroundings.

I remember that Herb kept bricks of cold chili in the fridge next to the stove. I can still see him dropping a brick into a big stew pot, adding water and some dry ingredients to form the ambrosia that we all knew and loved. I had always thought that Herb brewed his own chili, but Don Cox informs me that he actually bought the bricks from a meat packing house, probably the same place where he got the ground beef. I now know that at least part of the dry ingredients were cumin and rolled oats—the cumin to create the unique flavor and the rolled oats to make additional bulk in the stew. Someone, either the meat packing house or Herb himself, also added a bit of sugar. There is nothing like a bit of sugar in a salty dish to feed one's addiction to sweet, and addicted we were.

To finish your meal at Herb's you could have a big piece of Hazel's homemade pie, which she baked at their house and brought into the joint. My stomach still remembers the complete satisfaction of having dined on the chili or hamburgers topped off by cherry pie—now *that* was living!

Since we had relatives living in Sedan, Caney, and other points east, my parents would often be traveling in that direction. In Sedan there was Riney's grill, which was even smaller than Herb's joint, but also had good hamburgers. In Caney we could purchase a bag of a dozen hamburgers for $1.00 in a takeout place on Highway 166. We thought that was the best bargain around, and my parents seldom passed it up when on the way home from a visit with relatives.

For a more complete dining experience there was the Hilltop Cafe across from the grade school and next door to Clarence Marshall's gas station. Clarence was Herb's brother and since he sold Standard Oil Company gasoline, as did my dad, we would often loaf at the service station. Hilltop Cafe was our place for a treat if we were there at meal time. At the Hilltop you could get a breakfast of pancakes, either a stack or a short stack, with bacon and a hot beef sandwich for lunch. I could also order a grilled cheese sandwich with pickles and fries for variety. The Hilltop was a classy establishment, with booths and tables and a juke box playing the best of Bob Wills and His Texas Playboys. In the evenings you could order a full meal there. I remember the chicken-fried steaks and the Salisbury steaks. (It seems that I ate mostly beef while growing up, since chicken didn't appeal to me.)

Behind the Hilltop was a set of tourist cabins where transient laborers lived when working in the area. People who were building roads or harvesting grain made the Hilltop Cafe their dining room. This made the Hilltop into a small window on the outside world that was rare in Cedar Vale. I would seldom go into the Hilltop without seeing strangers eating and conversing there.

There was another eating establishment, Bernice and Charlie Donahue's Cafe, down on the corner of the main street and Highway 166, across from the bank. My mother considered that place to be a "house of ill repute" and would not allow my father to take me there. To my knowledge, I never crossed the threshold of the place, but it remains in my memory as a mysteriously attractive and forbidden domain where all sorts of illicit activities must have been taking place. I'm sure that those illicit activities, which probably had no basis in fact other than my mother's overactive imagination, would seem quite tame viewed from a twenty-first century perspective, but they certainly added to the flavor of the town I grew up in.

Visiting Grandparents

When I was growing up in Cedar Vale, Kansas, my parents and I visited with my grandparents nearly every weekend. Both sets of grandparents were living on farms outside of the neighboring county seat, Sedan. My father's parents lived on what was known as Moore Prairie, a flat limestone prairie that is somewhat bleak in appearance. My great-grandparents had homesteaded the farm in the late nineteenth century, and my grandfather had built the house and outbuildings over the years (see "The White Family of Moore Prairie, Kansas," p. 89). My mother's parents, the Call family, lived a few miles north and east of the White family, but their area was heavily wooded and had several small creeks that emptied into Caney River. That neighborhood was called the Rogers neighborhood and had had a one-room schoolhouse of that name in the time before the county schools were consolidated. Both of my parents had received their entire education to the eighth grade in one-room rural schoolhouses.

Our usual pattern was to visit each set of grandparents on alternating Sundays. There would always be a big Sunday dinner cooked on the wood stove in my grandmother White's kitchen or on the gas stove in my grandmother Call's kitchen. My maternal uncles had drilled for oil on the Call place and struck mostly gas, which they piped directly into the house. The Calls heated the house, cooked their food, and lighted the place entirely with natural gas from their own wells. My uncles also siphoned off what they called "casinghead gas," a liquid that they burned in their pickups. It was the first unleaded fuel, many years before it had been mandated by law. I shudder to think what safety and tax-law violations were occurring at the Call place.

The alternating Sundays couldn't have been more different for me. When we visited with the Whites I was the only child; none of my father's siblings had children. I was the apple of my grandparents' eyes and always treated with something special. When we arrived, Grandmother White would have hot rolls just out of the oven, which I soaked in her fresh-churned butter. I still remember the taste of those butter-ladened rolls and have never been able to duplicate the flavor.

On the alternating Sunday, when we visited the Calls, I was one of a half-dozen or more cousins since all of my mother's siblings had children. While I was not given the royal treatment there, I had the advantage of having several children my own age to play with. We roamed the woods and creeks around the farm, picked wild strawberries in season, and often got into poison ivy. Calamine lotion had been developed by that time and it was considered the best treatment for the affliction. I can't count the number of times I endured the terrible itching of poison ivy as I was growing up, and I was quite surprised to find that as an adult I seem to be immune to it. I've walked through poison ivy repeatedly and never have been infected with the itching rash.

On Sunday afternoons at the Whites the adult males played games like pitch or dominos. When I was old enough I joined in the games and enjoyed the banter of my grandfather, father, and my uncle Vernon as they teased each other as men are prone to do when playing games. I could also go to the parlor where my grandmother had an old reed organ. After I had begun piano lessons I could play hymns and familiar songs on that wheezy old instrument that was in doubtful tune. Sometimes I would go upstairs into the upper bedrooms, which were papered with old newspapers. I enjoyed reading the comics on the walls and developed a taste for the newspaper columns of Will Rogers (1879-1935), a humorist and sometimes movie actor of the 1920s and early 1930s. He had come from Oklahoma and often appeared with a lariat rope with which he did tricks while delivering a running satire on the events of the day. The newspaper columns on the walls were pretty much like the films of his live performances that I have seen, but, of course, they referred to events that took place before I was born. I remember several of Will Rogers' sayings. A typical example would be, "I belong to no organized political party—I'm a Democrat."

When we visited with the Calls, I would play with my cousins for most of the afternoon, but I always tried to spend some time sitting at Grandfather Call's feet. Mark Call was a deep thinker, an agnostic, and a socialist. He was also a pacifist and was totally against the war that was raging in Europe and Asia at the time. I can remember him saying that if Roosevelt had had to build all that war material to get us out of the Depression, well, he should have just taken it out to sea and sunk it there. Grandfather Call was a life-long Republican but not cut from the same cloth as the current crop of that political party. He was adamantly opposed to organized religion and detested capitalism in any form. I sometimes wonder what he would think of his Republican party as it is now structured.

All in all, I received a balanced view of the two political parties—Democrat on the Sundays reading the old newspapers at the Whites and Republican on the alternating Sundays sitting at Grandfather Call's feet. Most of all, I took in my grandfather Call's socialist, agnostic, pacifist views and made them my own. I thought that Grandfather Call was the smartest person alive and I absorbed everything he said. While I have considerably broadened my view of the world with the passing of time, I remember so clearly those Sunday afternoons sitting at Grandfather Call's feet. I still think he was a pretty wise old man and I would love to hear one of his monologues again, delivered by the light of a gas lamp next to the old gas stove in their ramshackle farm house in rural Chautauqua County, Kansas.

Tank Wagon Days

My most vivid memories of my father are riding along with him in his Standard Oil Company tank wagon delivering gasoline to farms in the Cedar Vale area. In the summer, when school was not in session, I would ride with him several times each week. When I was still too short to see out the front windshield, Dad put a can of axle grease on the passenger's seat for me to sit on. Sometimes on deserted country roads he would take me on his lap so I could "drive the truck" while he worked the pedals. What a feeling of power for a small boy to be in charge of that huge truck with hundreds of gallons of gas in the tanks behind! Later, when I was learning to drive, that early experience stood me in good stead, since guiding a vehicle was a skill I had already learned many years before.

Each stop along Dad's route was an adventure. Sometimes I was invited in by the farm wife to have a piece of pie or some bread and jelly while my dad carried pairs of five-gallon pails of gas to lift up over his head and pour into the farmer's tank. The top of these pails were partially open, forming a funnel-like arrangement. Delivering gas in the early days was very hard work because it was done by hand, but in later years Dad had a pump and hose arrangement installed so he could use the truck's engine to pump the fuel. There was a second small gear shift inside the truck that engaged a "power takeoff" to activate the pump. The fuel was metered with what looked like a miniature filling station pump, and Dad's job was to watch the meter and be sure to cut off the pump before the tank overflowed. On some occasions, when he would be visiting with the farmer, he missed getting the pump stopped in time and there would be a sudden flood. My dad constantly smelled of gasoline and I'm sure I did too. In those days, no one knew about the dangers of inhaling gasoline fumes. We all breathed in the fumes all the time. I can remember standing up on the tank wagon looking down into the huge tank as gasoline was pouring in.

Sometimes a farm would have a friendly dog or two that I could play with while waiting for Dad to finish his work, which always included a visit with the farmer if he was available. Sometimes there would be kids my age and I would join them in whatever they were doing. On more than one farm there was a girl who would take me behind the barn or to her room for a few stolen kisses and a different sort of play. I grew to look forward to some of the stops Dad would make, anticipating what activity might be in store there. I was quite precocious in developing a way with the girls.

My dad set a leisurely pace for his life. He always took time to visit at each farm, and the conversations would seem to go on for hours, although that would depend on how interesting my activities were. If I was having a good time the visit seemed all too short.

We would often make unscheduled stops when we were near a good fishing or swimming hole. Dad had two long cane poles on the tank at the back of the truck, and we would walk down to someplace on Cedar Creek and catch a few sunfish to throw back. A fishing break was never a time for serious fishing, since it would be too long before we would be home and the fish would spoil. We had a few favorite places along Cedar Creek that were not too deep and where the bottom was solid rock. We would park the truck and take off our clothes for skinny dipping to cool us off (see "Swimming," p. 165). Another favorite break was climbing up Lookout Mountain to visit the cave. I left secret messages in the cracks there and would see if they were still there when we next visited. My mother thought that Dad was pretty lazy because he took all that time to have fun, but those are my most treasured memories of the time I spent with him.

Dad would regale me with stories of growing up on the farm and his early days running a filling station in Sedan, Kansas. The filling station stories were my favorites, since a group of men had hung out at Dad's station and they were always playing practical jokes on each other. They all called each other by funny nicknames. Two of my favorite nicknames his cronies gave to my father are "Whipsnade" and "Whipple." I have no idea where these names came from, but I thought they were funny. An example of a practical joke would be placing mustard oil (a fatty oil obtained by pressing mustard seeds) on one of the chairs in the station and getting one of the guys to sit down in it. That would send the poor victim running for the nearest rest room to clean the noxious stuff off his bum and his pants. To hear my dad tell about the shenanigans of the group at the service station was great fun because he was clearly having a good time telling the stories. When my father was happy, which was quite often, he would do a little soft-shoe dance that he learned by mimicking Fred Astaire in the movies. He was also quite fond of singing, and we would sing a lot of the old songs he knew at the top of our lungs while driving along through the countryside.

My dad was a tolerant, easy-going man who wished no one harm. He was satisfied with his lot in life. When we were out on the tank wagon he was a lot of fun to be with, but he seemed to shut down as soon as we got home. Mother was what you would call "upwardly mobile." She was not satisfied with our lot and worked nonstop to improve it. I can say that I have lived my life much more along the lines of my mother, but now, since retirement, I am aiming to be much more like my father.

Taking Care of the Old Folks

My grandparents' 401K's were their children. As subsistence farmers there was no "retirement plan" in place and, as they aged and became infirm, their children gradually took over more and more of the farm operations.

In the case of my paternal grandparents their eldest daughter, my aunt Fern, stayed at home and assisted them for their entire life. In the final years of Grandfather White's life, I remember the Sundays when my father, my uncles Vernon and Charlie Smith, (a farmer married to my father's other sister, Sylvia), and I went into the woods to cut firewood for the grandparents. Charlie Smith had all the necessary tools, and we each took turns with the axes and saws and brought in enough wood to heat my grandparents' home for the entire winter. We also got together when it was butchering time so that the grandparents would have pork for the winter. Aunt Fern raised a huge garden and canned fruit and vegetables for their winter needs. When Grandfather White died in 1954, the children bought a house in Sedan for Grandmother and Fern. The sale of the farm provided their living, along with what Aunt Fern could bring in by cleaning houses in Sedan. Grandmother White died in 1964. Fern lived out the last of her years in that house. Her "retirement" was provided for by the savings she had accumulated in her earlier years as a cook and housekeeper, along with the house that was free and clear.

My maternal grandparents lived on their farm until Grandfather Call passed away in 1952. In his declining years he was helped out more and more by my uncle Harold, who lived with his family on a portion of the farm. After Grandfather Call's death, all the children got together and built Grandmother a little house in Sedan on the back of my uncle Lee's place. Her "retirement" was provided for by the sale of the farm and periodic contributions of food and money by all her children. When my uncle Lee moved from his home around 1960, the remaining children bought a small trailer home for Grandmother Call and she lived out her final years until her death in 1973 in that trailer, which was always parked near one of her childrens' homes.

In my parents' generation, regular retirement programs were available. Both of my parents retired from their employment with pensions. My father drew a regular pension from the Standard Oil Company (AMOCO, now British Petroleum) and my mother drew a pension from the telephone company, ATT (now broken up into regional divisions). In addition, they had participated in employee stock plans with Standard Oil and ATT. I was freed from supporting them. I served as financial manager of their assets after my father's death in 1991. At that time Mother moved to Ames, Iowa, where I was teaching, and we set her up in a retirement community. This gave her independence and medical support when her health declined in the last two years of her life. Mother died in November 1998 after a series of strokes, two months after the death of Elyn's mother, also of a stroke.

Elyn's parents were in a similar situation to my parents. They both retired with pensions from Iowa State University and moved to a retirement community in San Diego, California. They had also engaged in regular savings during their employment years, and they had assets that could be used to supplement their pensions. The retirement community provided day-to-day support as needed. Our role was as financial manager of their assets after Elyn's mother died in 1998. Elyn's father continued to live in his cottage in the retirement community until his death in 2006. In his declining years, Elyn took on the role of care manager, watching out for his medical needs from wherever we happened to be living by daily phone conversations and frequent visits. The health-care system in southern California was not as reliable as the system in central Iowa, and regular oversight was needed to ensure that he had the care he needed.

Elyn and I are now engaged in our own financial planning so that we can live comfortably without needing financial support from our children in our declining years. I had a regular retirement program in my employment at Iowa State University and, in addition, engaged in regular saving. Assets inherited from our parents supplement our income along with royalties from the sale of our books. How we will deal with the increasing need for care in our declining years remains to be seen. At least we have long-term-care insurance to take over some of the possible financial burden of those years.

As I look at the next generation, I see quite a different pattern emerging. Fewer and fewer companies have regular retirement programs, and young people seem to move from job to job and are much more often self employed. The entire burden of saving for retirement is increasingly placed in their laps. Are they saving? The statistics are not promising. Will their "retirement programs" again be the responsibility of their children? Will "extended family" again be a living pattern for them? Only time will tell how the next generation of "old folks" will be cared for in their declining years. The Social Security system doesn't look like a good bet as a source of significant income.

The wheels of time turn; there will always be a generation of "old folks" to be cared for. I'm sure they will work it out some way. People have always managed to figure it out.

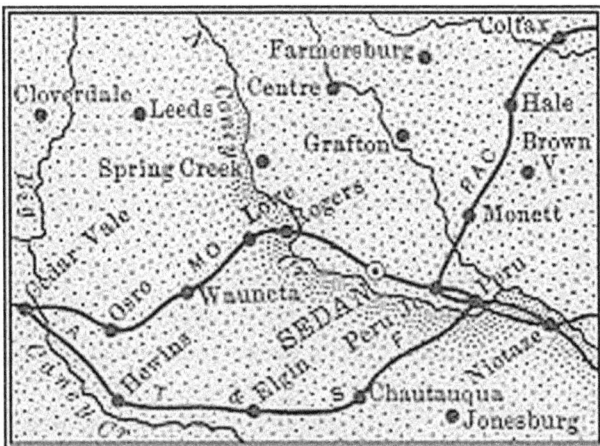

1899 Map of Chautauqua
County, Kansas

Climbing a 14er

It was the year between finishing my Master's degree at the University of Kansas and beginning my Ph.D. studies at Michigan State University. I took a year off to teach in the public schools in Dolores, Colorado, a tiny mountain town tucked deep inside the Dolores River canyon in the southwestern corner of the state. During this year I met David , the pastor of the local Methodist Church. David had been a student of Paul Tillich, the great Christian existential philosopher at Harvard. What David was doing in this small mountain town was a mystery. Perhaps the Methodist Church needed a place to hide some-one of his radical persuasion, or perhaps David simply wanted to live in the Rocky Mountains. In any event, David was intellectually so far above the members of that small congregation that they never once noticed that his prayers didn't end with "in Jesus' name" and phrases such as "Lord and Savior" never passed his lips. He was a Methodist pastor whom an agnostic like me could get close to, and I agreed to sing in his church choir although I did turn down the opportunity to lead it.

I enjoyed David's sermons, which were beautiful essays on ethics and humanism. Even my Grandfather Call would have been happy with his preaching. I remember that Grandfather had once told the local minister that he would only come to church the Sunday that he preached of "man's duty to man" instead of "man's duty to God." Grandfather Call proudly said that he had never had to make good on that promise. David became my best friend and confidant during my one year in Dolores.

Along with being an intellectual of major accomplishment, David was an avid mountain climber. He had been an instructor in technical climbing in a mountaineering school earlier in his life. Early in the fall, David hatched a plan that we would climb one or two of the fourteen-thousand-foot peaks in the Dolores range, just north and east of town. That was a huge challenge for both of us since I had never been at all athletic and was not particularly confident of my abilities as a mountain climber. The challenge for David was to bring me up to a level where he could get me up and down the mountain in one piece.

David was the most patient teacher I have ever met. He began by taking me out on short hikes, increasing the distance and challenge by easy degrees. He was always instructing me about climbing safety, showing me how to tell if an avalanche or rock fall was imminent and how to traverse loose rock fields safely. He taught me the basics of rappelling over cliffs on a rope and how to belay a partner in dangerous situations. He told me about the dangers of euphoria due to oxygen starvation at high altitudes and how to know when and where to take cover in case of sudden thunderstorms. The result was that I actually felt ready to attempt a 14er by the spring and, when it was safe to do so, we made our plans to climb Mt. Wilson in the Dolores Peaks.

We picked a beautiful sunny Saturday in the late spring and made our ascent. The plan was to drive high enough up the mountain that we could make the entire climb in one day and David could be back in time for his sermon on Sunday. If you haven't actually climbed a 14er, words can hardly convey the experience. If you have climbed one, you will already know what I'm attempting to describe.

In the first place, the climb is very strenuous and you have to pace yourself very carefully. The rest breaks and taking in food and water must be carefully planned so that you can be at the summit before the afternoon thunderstorms move in. Being on top of one of the highest mountain peaks in the Rocky Mountains in a thunderstorm can be deadly, and many climbers have been struck by lightning. David was impeccable in pacing us and circumventing dangers from falling rocks and sliding snow. In due course, we made the summit.

Standing on the summit of a fourteen-thousand-foot mountain is one of life's peak experiences. All during the ascent I was looking at the face of the mountain, walking over huge fields of loose rock with the sound of mountain streams underfoot. There are often mountain streams, fed by snow melt, running through the rock fields high in the mountains. When the summit was achieved the whole 360-degree panorama suddenly opened up around me and I could see forever in all directions. I was literally standing on top of the world. I knew I must be short of oxygen because I had an overwhelming desire to just stay there. My judgment was so impaired that David had to be quite stern with me when it was time to start down.

The trip down the mountain was just as strenuous as the ascent. We took the easy way of sliding down snow fields whenever possible, but, even so, my knees took a beating. By the time we were back at the pickup I was almost unconscious from sheer fatigue. I hardly remember the trip home. However, in the days and years following, I have continued to savor every moment of that beautiful day. I remember my friend and teacher David with great love and affection. We made other climbs together and they were beautiful experiences, but that first day of standing on the top of the world will always be the day I remember.

Becoming Nobody

"I'm nobody! Who are you?
Are you nobody, too?"
Emily Dickinson

Having made the choice in the early 1990s to retire from university teaching, I looked forward to the freedom to pursue all the new directions that were beckoning to me. My burgeoning interest in spiritual practice was very attractive; my interest in alternative healing practices was just beginning (see "Body Work," p. 121); and I had a new and exciting partner for all the coming adventures. I cleared out the residue of my previous life and moved in with my new wife and partner, Elyn. We shared a tiny student apartment on the campus of Iliff School of Theology at Denver University where Elyn was a student.

Suddenly it seemed I had lost my identity. Elyn's fellow students were friendly enough, but I was accustomed to being treated as "Dr. White, Distinguished Professor" and that wasn't who I was any more. I experienced an emptiness that I hadn't anticipated. I didn't want to be "Dr. White" any more, but that raised the question of who I was going to be in this new life.

Elyn was busy in her student life at Iliff School of Theology. She was a full-time student studying to be a Unitarian Universalist minister. Her naturally gregarious nature made her a popular and active student in the Iliff family. She had a full life there—and I had a lot of time on my hands. I tried reading and began to do some writing (early drafts of some of the pieces in this book were written at that time). I had some ongoing work associated with my textbooks (see "How I Became an Author," p. 32), but I also had a lot time on my hands. In leaving Ames, Iowa, I had not only left behind my university colleagues and the status of my position but also a circle of close friends with whom I had spent considerable time. I was experiencing a crisis that I had not anticipated—the proverbial "identity crisis."

This crisis lasted for several years. I got used to not being deferred to ("Yes sir, Dr. White") and not having a hardworking staff at my disposal, but there was a hole in my psyche that I couldn't seem to fill. If any of my readers are contemplating retirement from an active career, I give you fair warning to expect a crisis of identity and a period of adjustment. I found ways to fill my time, but there was an underlying depression that I couldn't seem to shake. I wish I could give you a formula for relieving that depression, but I can only say that it gradually cleared and I began to explore who I really was when the position and status were gone. I can say that ongoing work on projects was an important part of how I got through that time, and I soon found interesting spiritual paths to pursue that opened new vistas for exploration. I found people that I wanted to spend time with. We spent a year living in Spain (see "In a Little Spanish Town . . .", p. 10) and walked the Camino de Santiago. I got used to the feeling of being "nobody" important. When people asked me "What do you do?" I got over the feelings of guilt at not having a pat answer. I began to say "I am living my life," or "I'm having fun." I no longer felt the need to trot out a list of my past achievements to justify my occupying space on this planet.

Gradually, over a period of years, I have come to see that my task for this part of my life is the challenge of becoming who I really am and of exploring who I want to be in the final stages of this journey. More and more I am trying to become transparent to myself and to others. This little book is a part of that process. After a lifetime of hiding behind various masks, I am working to put all of the parts of myself together and to feel comfortable in letting others know me (see "Picking Up the Pieces," p. 151). I have recently started a blog with a group of my old high-school classmates and I am enjoying getting to know them again. I am gradually opening up all the areas of my life to them and enjoy shocking some of them from time to time.

In this journey I am blessed to have a partner who is willing to grow with me, to cajole me when I am not present to her, and who is blessed with the sweetest disposition I could imagine. She is truly my partner on all of life's paths and when I get up the courage to reveal more of myself she is always there, cheering me on. Now you know why I have dedicated this slim volume to her. It is a small token of the gratitude I feel for my beloved partner, Elyn Aviva.

Another Ghost Story

My second encounter with the unknown forces that are often called "ghosts" (see "A Ghost Story," p. 157) occurred in the late 1990s when my beloved Elyn and I purchased a house in the south part of Boulder, Colorado. This house trailed down four levels over a bluff overlooking a public park with views out to the Front Range of the Rocky Mountains from every level. It was more house than we needed, but the natural beauty that met the eye in every room was quite seductive to us. The house had recently been remodeled, with a new kitchen and refurbished bathrooms, so all we had to do was paint, replace the carpet, and move in.

Elyn had done all the preliminary searching for a house and when she had it narrowed to three choices, I took a look at all of them. I was immediately attracted to the views from this house and chose it. Housing was selling rapidly and this house had not yet appeared on the Boulder Multiple Listing, so I knew we had to move at once. We made an offer before they held an open house and it was accepted by the owner.

As we revisited the house Elyn began to have second thoughts. She sensed that there was something wrong there. Hearing the story of the previous owners, who had divorced after a crib death, just confirmed her suspicions. I, on the other hand, had just put down several thousand dollars of earnest money and was not about to lose it. Friends told Elyn that once we had redecorated and done a thorough house cleansing it would be just fine.

My first indication that all might not be well with the house was at the closing when we were to take possession. The previous owner, a woman we had barely met, became quite unnerved at giving up possession of the house. She wept and made several accusations about how her realtor had not given her accurate information concerning a penalty for paying off her mortgage. There were heated conferences held out in the hall. She finally came back and signed the necessary documents and we were the official owners. After we moved in and got to know the neighbors, we began to hear stories of how she had been a difficult and hysterical neighbor to deal with and how glad they were to have us in the neighborhood. All this confirmed our experience at the closing, but we took little notice of it as we arranged our things and got to know our new house.

The arrangement of the house was unusual in that the master bedroom was on the lowest floor of the house. This bedroom was connected to a family room, which looked out on an extensive balcony. The laundry room and a small study were also on this level. In a loft area over the family room were three rooms, which became a TV room, my massage room, and my office. The floor above (which was actually at street level) contained the living room, dining room, and kitchen, and Elyn had her office spaces on the top floor of the house, giving us the separate work spaces that we prefer.

In the middle of the night, several months after we moved into the house, the TV in the room above our bedroom suddenly turned itself on at full volume. I ran upstairs and turned it off and went back to bed. We thought that the cable company must have been reprogramming their system and had accidently turned the set on. Several weeks later, the same thing happened. We were annoyed, but again attributed it to the cable company. When we began to be awakened fairly regularly I turned off the cable box and that seemed to cure the problem.

We also became aware of a strange smell in the TV room. We thought that perhaps the 100% wool carpet we had installed all over the house had somehow taken on moisture. We tried various deodorizing techniques, but the smell never left. It was never overwhelming, and I could spend time there watching TV, but Elyn just didn't like being in that room.

Several years later, during a visit by a woman who had helped us with Feng Shui in the house, we commented on the smell in that room. She walked into the room and immediately identified the smell as sour baby formula. She thought that the ghost of the baby who had died of SIDS in the house might be stuck in the room. I was very doubtful of this analysis, but the room had, indeed, been the nursery where the baby had died.

Elyn went into action. She called in several friends to help her clear out the baby ghost. Several methods were tried, all without success.

Next, I went into action. I decided to move my massage room into this space and put the TV in another room in the house. As preparation for this move, I ran an essential-oil nebulizer continuously for about a week and played massage music twenty-four hours a day in the space. I then moved my massage equipment into the space and I thought I had cleared the place of any wandering spirit that might have been trapped there. It, indeed, seemed that all was OK but then I noticed that if I smelled very carefully around the door leading out of the house from this room, I could still detect the same sour baby odor. If I didn't run the essential oil nebulizer for several days, the odor would begin to creep back into the space. For the remaining time that we lived in this house I did constant battle with this smelly baby ghost. I could keep it confined to the doorway, but could never totally eliminate it.

Once the TV was out of the haunted room it never again came on in the middle of the night. We lived with the baby ghost for a few more months and decided that this place was not for us. We were able to sell the house without any trouble, since it had terrific views of the mountains. As a final gesture for the new owners, we called on a professional "ghost buster" who worked by telephone. That finally cleared the room and we felt it was safe to pass it on to the new owners and their young children.

I had occasion to visit the place about a year after we had left and could detect no odor or anything unusual in the space. I think the baby ghost had, indeed, gone "back to the light" or wherever baby ghosts go. May she rest in peace.

Dentistry in Cedar Vale

Cedar Vale was served by two dentists, Herb and Josh Stone. Josh was Herb's father and, by the time I was growing up, he was partially retired. That meant that he was working somewhat shorter hours than Herb, who was in the office nearly day and night. The Stone office was a complete dentistry, encompassing the usual drilling, filling, and extractions. In addition, the Stones made all their own bridgework and dentures on-site. The two dentists worked alone without support staff. No one met you at the door and no one billed you for the work that was done. I would add that no one ever cleaned the office, to my knowledge, and dust bunnies grew unimpeded in every corner. The laboratory room where dentures and bridgework were made was in total chaos and just as dirty as the waiting room. The operatory where the dreaded dental chair was installed was little better than the rest of the office. Herb and Josh Stone were old-fashioned dentists who worked with their bare hands and in street clothes. They probably washed their hands between patients, and there was a sterilizer in the back room, but instruments were laid out on a circular glass tray that was as dusty as everything else in the office.

You might think that the office would have been the absolute epicenter for disease transmission in Cedar Vale, but I never remember any of the Stone's patients catching any terrible disease from being treated there. I have a personal theory about that. I believe that we were all living in a very small, isolated island in the middle of the prairies, and we were sharing our space with an equally small band of microbe strains that coursed through all our systems and against which we all had excellent immune defenses. My guess is that we couldn't pick up anything from Herb Stone's unsterile office that we weren't exposed to on the streets of the town every day.

When a patient required the complete extraction of all teeth in preparation for dentures (a common practice in those days), those operations were performed under a general anesthetic in nearby Hays Hospital. The story that I heard from my mother, who was a telephone operator and knew everything that was going on in town, was that Herb Stone would be met at the door of the hospital and his instruments would be confiscated to be sterilized before going into the surgery. Herb was then required to wear rubber gloves and hospital scrubs for the operation, an inconvenience that he must have hated. (One of my CV bloggers claims this is a false story. Who knows.)

The dentistry practiced in Cedar Vale was very simple. We were encouraged to brush our teeth regularly, but no one had ever heard of tarter removal or regular dental cleaning. You went to the dentist when you thought you needed to, with pain often being the first symptom. Herb and Josh drilled and filled teeth using the mercury amalgam that is still used by traditional dentists. I remember Herb rolling and shaping the mercury/silver mixture between his fingers before inserting it into the cavity he had just drilled. The amount of mercury exposure he endured on a daily basis must have been enormous, but he showed no ill effects. When a tooth could not be saved by filling, it was usually extracted. The gap might be filled with a bridge or simply left to take care of itself if the patient couldn't afford that expense. When enough gaps appeared in one's smile, all the teeth were extracted and a full denture was created.

When I was a junior in high school one of my front teeth simply died. I can remember getting it bumped in the middle of a football marching band show; in a few days I had an abscessed tooth. The tooth in question was the upper tooth next to the front teeth (number 7 for those of you who know the system for numbering teeth). Normally that would have resulted in my having the tooth extracted, but Herb knew that I was "first-chair trumpet" in the band and needed that tooth to be able to play. He consulted with Josh. Together they undertook to do a root canal filling, which was not part of their usual practice.

They decided to both work on my tooth, and for several weeks I had almost daily appointments with one or another of them. I won't bore you with the gory details, but in a few weeks the job was complete and that root canal has lasted until the present time. The tooth in question has now been crowned to look like a new tooth, but the root canal that Herb Stone put in over fifty years ago is still there and never causes me a moment's trouble. And that was done in an office that was never cleaned, using instruments that were probably not sterile. It is enough to test one's faith in the microbe theory of disease transmission.

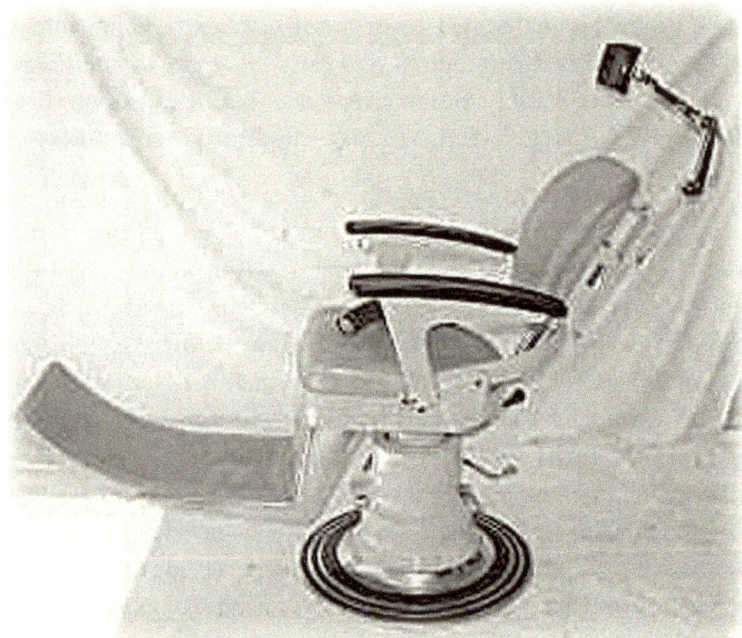

The White Family of Moore Prairie, Kansas

Moore Prairie Cemetery in rural Chautauqua County, Kansas, lists sixteen deceased occupants with the name of White. All of these people are relatives of mine. How this came to be centers around one rather shadowy individual, my great-grandfather, Caleb White (1839-??).

Caleb and his new wife, Eliza Head White (1839-1920), arrived in New York from Liverpool, England, on June 22, 1864. Life in England had been hard for Caleb. In the 1851 British Census twelve-year-old Caleb was listed as the only offspring of Samuel and Philadelphia White, who are identified as "Paupers—formerly farmers." How Caleb met Eliza and when they were married is unknown, but there is little doubt about their reasons for leaving England for the New World. The abject poverty they must have experienced and the lure of opportunities in the New World must have been overwhelming.

The Whites began the move west along with that steady flood of immigrants who were seeking a better life in the U.S. They must have taken several years to reach Kansas because their first two children Philadelphia (1865) and Samuel Fredrick (1867) were born in Illinois. By 1870 they had homesteaded on Moore Prairie and little Alice was born. My grandfather, Howard Charles, was born in 1872, and Daisy in 1876. Shortly afterwards, Caleb apparently just up and left, leaving Eliza alone in the wilds of frontier Kansas with five small children.

Those of us who muck about among dead folk searching for our connections to European royalty are bound to turn up a few pitiful characters and an occasional scoundrel. Caleb White may fit into both of those categories. Eliza was later known in the family for her sharp tongue; whether that came before or after Caleb left I don't know. Anyway, Eliza gathered up her little band of farmhands and, by God, made a go of it on the homestead on Moore Prairie. Philadelphia became "Della" and Samuel Fredrick became "Fred," thus erasing any connection with Caleb's parents in England. Eliza seems to have been determined to start all over again in her adopted country, and she systematically cleared Caleb White out of her life.

I heard two pieces of family folklore about Caleb from my father. One was that Caleb had been a sailor and found life away from the sea onerous. I have always doubted that bit of folklore, considering that his parents before him had been failed farmers and every census record I've found shows that he listed his occupation as farmer. My guess was that that excuse was made up by Eliza as a cover for the real reasons that Caleb left. However, when the Whites came into New York on the Progress from Liverpool in 1864, Caleb lists his occupation as mariner. So there may be some truth to that family story. The other story is that several years after Caleb took off he returned, and Eliza ran him off the place. Now that fits with what I know about my great-grandmother and tends to confirm Caleb's status as ne'er-do-well.

By 1885 the White family was quite grown up. Della, age 20, was listed as a housekeeper; Fred, age 18, is a farmer; Alice, age 15, is listed for housework; and Howard, age 12, is a farmer. Only little Daisy, age 9, has no listed occupation. They started working young, these Whites. That is quite consistent with the picture my father painted of the family. He described the Whites as a family with grim determination, tolerating no nonsense or fun. This shaped my grandfather's character; I remember him as a rather bleak character who just wouldn't stop working, even after a botched prostate surgery left him incontinent and weakened. My father said that he had had a similar upbringing to his father. If there was an easy way and a hard way to do anything, his father always chose the hard way. That my father didn't pass that same grim determination on to me and didn't live his own life that way is a tribute to his ability to rise above his upbringing. Perhaps he was just as determined to have some fun in life because of what he experienced growing up.

My grandfather's brother, Fred, grew up and married Hannah (1875-1949). They built a place of their own on part of the homestead. There they raised seven children, Ray A. (1900-1959), Ralph L. "Boots" (1901-1971), Orville (1905-1948), Ward L. (1907-1997), Lynn (1909-1970), Thelma (1913-??), and Buel O. (1915-1974). What a bunch of farmers they must have been. For the most part, all of these children farmed in the Moore Prairie area, and all of them procreated, thus accounting for a good part of the list of White occupants in Moore Prairie Cemetery.

My grandfather, Howard Charles (1872-1954) was the fourth child of Eliza and Caleb. He married Mary Florence Witham (1876-1964) and they had four children: H. Fern (1903-1989); Sylvia O. (1908-2001); my father, Charles Howard (1911-1991); and Vernon D. (1915-1973). Eliza lived with this family until her death in 1920. The H. C. White family was not prolific. Fern never married; Sylvia married Charlie Smith, but they had no children; my father married Lila B. Call and I was their only child; and Vernon married later in life and had no children. I was the only "next generation" (see "Visiting Grandparents," p. 68). So, while all the Whites of Moore Prairie were and are relatives of mine, few are what I would consider close relatives. However, we all carry some of that Moore Prairie limestone in our bones and have all been hard workers all our lives.

Composing I

The Beginning

I began composing as soon as I began piano lessons at about age eight. I wrote little pieces for my piano teacher, Mrs. Kirby (see "Bertha Kirby," p. 112). Making up my own music seemed as natural to me as playing someone else's music. When I began to play the trumpet, I began to play by ear. My father would come home and say, "Play Stardust for me." I'd have to find the notes on my horn, and, after much trial and error, I became quite good at it. I could play along with songs on the radio and even add my own embellishments. My early interest in jazz (see "Listening to Jazz on a Saturday Night," p. 109), contributed to my creative development. At the same time that I was learning to play by note in the band, I was constantly improvising at home and at school.

My active interest in composition came when I attended Midwestern Music and Art Camp at the University of Kansas. At the camp I heard a live symphony orchestra for the first time. I said to Becky Grantham, my girlfriend at camp that summer, "Some day I'll write music for symphony orchestra." I'm sure she thought I was just day-dreaming, but she went along with me. I returned home from camp that summer sure that my destiny was to be a composer.

When I enrolled at KU in the fall of 1955 as a music education major, my first required classes were harmony, sight-singing and ear training, and keyboard harmony. I took to the harmony class like a duck to water. By the second year my little compositions, which Mr. Ledwith required of all students, were often played in class as outstanding examples of how the assignments could be done creatively. Mr. Ledwith recognized that I had talent, and he took me to meet Mr. Anderson, the head of composition and organ in the school. Mr. Anderson liked what he saw and accepted me as a private student in composition. For two years I was the only music education major who was studying composition. In my junior year I declared myself as a double major in music education and music composition. I hoped to be able to finish both majors within the four years, but that proved impossible, since a full year of counterpoint and a senior recital was required to complete the music composition degree. I finished the music education degree, taught for a year in the public schools in Hoxie, Kansas, and returned to KU to complete the composition degree.

The University of Kansas had a very strange approach to their music education major. For the first two years students were in the School of Music and for the final two years they were in the School of Education. A real turf battle went on between the two areas, and they scarcely spoke to each other. Since I was in the School of Education for the final two years, all the classes related to my composition major had to be approved by my advisor, who was a music educator. For the most part, that was no problem—I could take as many additional classes as I wanted so long as I was making progress toward the Mus. Ed. degree. There was, however, one class that caused me considerable difficulty. The composition major required a class in orchestration, while the Mus. Ed. degree required a class in music arranging for instrumental ensembles. The content of the two classes was quite similar, but neither the School of Music or School of Education would accept the other's class as equivalent. I petitioned the School of Education to allow me to take the orchestration class in lieu of the music arranging class. This caused considerable upheaval and I was called in to talk with the chairman of music education, E. Thayer Gaston. He grilled me for over half an hour about why I did not want to take "their" class. In the end he relented and I took the orchestration class.

There are two ironies for me in this situation. I had a classmate in music education, Claude T. Smith, who took the arranging class that I had waived. As a final project he wrote a quick-step march for band that was so good that the KU Band premiered it in one of their concerts. This was the beginning of his long career as a composer of works for school band that included well over one hundred pieces. His works are still in the repertoire of school bands all over the U.S. Claude was a much more successful composer than I ever was, measured by income generated and the recognition of the public, and he never took a composition class in his life! The other irony is that many years later I wrote *Instrumental Arranging,* a textbook for the class I had waived.

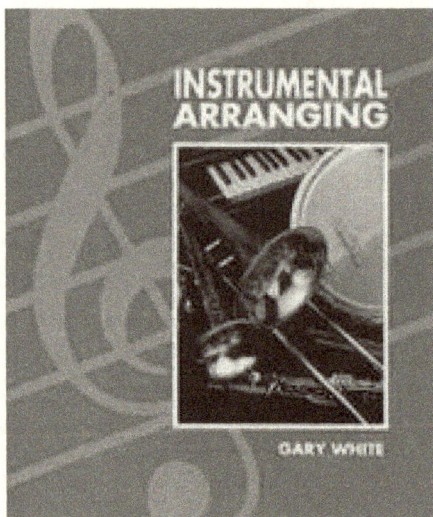

Composing II

The Process

I have always found that the best ideas, the real substance of a composition, come from the area of my mind that can't be commanded directly. It is that "subconscious," or "right brain," or whatever you choose to call it that can be coaxed or bidden but never ordered. I know that the left and right brain theory, in which the left brain takes care of verbal and related functions and the right brain does the creative stuff, has been pretty well shot down in recent years, but I'll continue to use the terminology anyway. (The brain is now seen as much more "holographic," with all parts participating together.) My trick for having a good idea for a piece was to get that part of my mind in the "right frame" and then to "listen."" I've developed and learned a number of techniques for making that happen.

In my first years of serious compositional study I practiced a form of self hypnosis that I had learned from a book. I would put myself into a light trance and make the suggestion that I would have a good musical idea. Then I'd wait to "hear" what happened and note it down. Sometimes idle improvising at the keyboard would help that process. Once I had the "idea," which might be a melody, some harmony, or even just a rhythm, I could begin to work with it and develop it using the skills I was learning in the composition class—how to extend and play out variations on my idea to make it into a complete piece of music. The self-hypnosis method I just described was my own invention. No composition teacher I ever studied with dealt with the fundamental process of having a good musical idea. The lessons were entirely about how to develop an idea into a complete composition.

In later years I often used visualization to "trick" the right brain into coming up with an idea. I would imagine as strongly as possible that I was attending the first performance of the piece I was beginning to write. The performers would come on stage, the audience would applaud, and they would prepare to play the piece. When the performance began, the music was always there, supplied by my subconscious—which seems to abhor a vacuum. Try it yourself and you'll see that it works. Again, this method was never taught to me by anyone. I did, however, teach it to all my own students and I offer it to you free of charge. Worth the price of the book!

I also used "dream time" to work on musical ideas. I would lay the groundwork, much as described above, just before going to bed. If I was in the middle of a piece, I would look through it to the point I had left off and then just go to sleep and see what developed. I have found that the subconscious mind never sleeps. It will continue chewing on an idea all through the night. More often than not I would wake up with the continuation or the beginning of the piece running in my head.

This process works for nearly any creative process. In writing these little essays I nearly always sleep on the idea before beginning to write anything down. Generally, I will have two or three topics that I want to write about and I'll see what comes clear in the night. Sometimes I wake in the middle of the night with the idea becoming so clear in my mind that I have to get up and write it down on the spot. This pattern had become such a habit in my years of serious compositional work that I still wake up around 3 a.m. and often get up to work awhile before returning to sleep.

In writing these little pieces, as in writing a composition, once the ideas are generated, the rest becomes mechanics. In the case of these essays, the mechanics consist of ordering the ideas; finding the right words to express them; composing the details of sentence structure, grammar, spelling, and punctuation. In the case of a musical composition it is much the same: musical setting (accompaniment, connecting sections, etc.) followed by the mechanics of music notation, orchestration, etc.

Doing these essays is like creating little one- and two-minute compositions. They are fun to do and don't involve the serious work that a more extended narrative (or musical composition) would require. I'm simply not in the mood for serious work these days.

I would encourage you to adapt the techniques I've described here to any creative work you may be engaged in. I predict that you will be very happy with the results.

Composing III

The Business

Once a composer has a piece of music finished the task becomes how to get a performance—or THE performance of one's dreams. Next is the question of how to be compensated for all the hours of work that go into producing a piece of music. Both of these tasks are what I'm calling "the business of music."

How to get a piece performed was a major problem early in my career before I had a reputation as a composer. The strategy I evolved was that I would approach a friend about writing a piece for them to perform, perhaps in their senior or graduate recital. This generally worked out well for both parties. The friend got to do a premiere in his or her senior recital and I was assured of getting a performance. Getting performances of small ensemble pieces could generally be handled in the same way. Most graduation recitals have some chamber music in them, and friends were generally grateful for my efforts. However, getting performances of my compositions for orchestra, band, or chorus was simply out of the question.

Later in life, when my reputation was secure, getting performances became very easy. I would simply tell a performer or a conductor that I was considering writing a piece for them and they were generally very happy to do the premiere performance. There is some difference among various ensembles as to their willingness to premiere new works. The difference, in my experience, is mostly a matter of how much literature is available for a given medium. For example, the orchestral literature is vastly larger than the concert-band literature, so orchestra conductors are less hungry for new works than band conductors. The same can be said for the string quartet vs. the brass quintet. When I look at my total output it seems to be proportioned along these lines. I wrote more band music than orchestral music and more music for wind ensembles than string quartets.

Although I was often able to arrange for the premiere performance of my compositions, that still left the question of the second, third, and fourth performances. That is a problem that all composers face and I was no exception. I generally found that the ensembles and instruments with smaller repertoire provided me with many more repeat performances than media with larger repertoire. An extreme case will illustrate the point.

Early in my career I was approached by Ronald Barnes, the carillonneur at the University of Kansas at the time, about writing a piece for him. (In case you don't know what carillon is, think "bell tower.") This came at a time when I was still having to approach performers to get performances rather than having them approaching me. The carillon had a very small repertoire at that time, and carillonneurs were searching for someone willing to write for them. I wrote about ten compositions for carillon and all of them are still being played today. When I get my quarterly statement from ASCAP (American Society of Composers, Authors, and Publishers) the performances listed will be predominantly those ten carillon pieces. They are performed widely in the U.S. and abroad and my foreign royalties are entirely due to those ten works. I was even honored by winning a competition in Holland for one of these works (see "Winning Prizes," p. 55).

All of which brings up the second question: how to be compensated for one's work. There are, of course, many non-monetary compensations for creating a piece of music. There is the personal satisfaction of hearing one's creation performed, the adulation one may receive from audiences, and recognition through prizes and awards.

However, turning a composition into actual financial profit is the kind of compensation I am addressing here.

One source of income from composing is commissions. An individual or an agency such as a foundation contracts with a composer to produce a piece of music. The money is normally paid half on signing the contract and half on delivery of the piece. The commissioning fee does not give the commissioning agency the copyright for the work. It guarantees the agency the right to the first performance and that the composition will be identified on the score and in program notes for all performances as having been commissioned by that agency. In the latter part of my productive life as a composer I worked primarily on commission. The commissioning fee is never large enough to compensate for the many hours of work involved in producing a large work, but it is a reliable source of income. A commission is somewhat like the advance publishers sometimes pay on a book project. The advance supports the author during the writing, but the real profits come if the published book sells.

A second source of income is from prizes. There are numerous competitions for compositions and a variety of prizes offered. Sometimes the prize includes a cash payment plus a public performance in a professional venue. Other times there may be only a guarantee of publication of the piece or there may be both a cash prize and publication. I would estimate that I received fewer than a dozen prizes for my compositions. When I was able to get commissions I stopped entering my compositions in prize competitions (see "Winning Prizes," p. 55). Commissioned works are often not accepted in prize competitions.

A third source of income is royalties. If a piece is published there will be royalties paid on the sale of the printed music. This amounts to around 10% of the retail price of the music. In my experience royalties are as often left unpaid as paid. Getting publishers to actually pay the agreed-upon royalties requires some persistence. Reputable publishers are quite regular in paying royalties on an annual or semi-annual basis, but there are many less reputable publishers who have to be reminded to pay up.

A fourth source of income is from performance fees. Performance of music in public or on the media (radio, television, film, etc.) is subject to fees. These fees are collected by agencies such as ASCAP and BMI (Broadcast Music Incorporated). Composers sign with one of these agencies and agree that they will be the sole licensing agency for performances of their work. In my case, I chose ASCAP as my licensing agency. Several times each year ASCAP sends me a check for all the performances of my work. In actual fact, however, no one is keeping track of each and every performance of anyone's music. ASCAP collects a blanket license fee from concert venues, radio and TV stations, bars, clubs, and restaurants and samples the performances in each area. This sample is used to distribute the license fees to composers. Each time one of my works is logged in the sample a number of points is generated. ASCAP assigns the value in dollars for each point and pays on that basis. The agencies are required by law to distribute all monies they take in, minus the cost of running the agency.

In addition, composers who achieve international recognition are sometimes paid for appearing at events. A contract is drawn for a fee to be paid for appearing, giving a lecture, conducting the work, performing, or whatever the agency requires of the composer. In my case, the fees were never much more than the cost of travel, meals, and lodging, but "star" composers (think Leonard Bernstein, Andrew Lloyd Weber, Phillip Glass, John Williams, and the like) can sometimes generate substantial fees for their appearance at events.

The largest source of compensation for my work as a composer was my university salary. All of my creative work and the public recognition it generated were considered in awarding academic promotions. With each promotion came an increase in salary. It was the total of all my creative work that gained me the rank of Distinguished Professor.

As you can see, the business of being a composer is vastly different from the creative process itself. I've known successful composers of only moderate talent who were very good at self promotion. I've also seen the reverse, where a composer of great ability can't achieve success in the marketplace because of an inability to promote his or her works. I think I was moderately talented and used my university position to good advantage in promoting my works.

The whole question of whether to try to make a career as a composer outside of the university is one that I seemed to have given little thought to. Perhaps it was my early life, growing up in rural southern Kansas, that kept me from even considering the "big time" of New York or Hollywood. I was too much of a "small town boy" to be comfortable living in the Big Apple. That would have been too fast a crowd for a guy from Cedar Vale, Kansas, and I knew it.

I also knew that it is very difficult for composers who are married and have families to make it in New York or Hollywood. In my generation, most successful New York composers were gay, and my married status would not have given me entrée into that world. As a family man I would not have given serious consideration to the life as a starving artist waiting tables in New York while waiting for my chance at the big premiere that would launch my career. University teaching was quite secure and fairly easily obtained in my generation, and I took that relatively easier route. I don't know if there are any "easy" routes for young composers today.

Weather

Weather was always an important factor in Cedar Vale, Kansas. In summer the heat and humidity were stifling, and in winter the ice storms would sometimes shut down the town completely. In my memory, the weather was seldom ideal for very long.

Kansas weather was always a subject for conversation wherever I went. Of course, farmers were always at the mercy of the weather —I can't remember any year that was great for putting the crops in, cultivating them, and harvesting. I heard a lot about the weather while traveling from farm to farm with my father on his Standard Oil Company tank wagon. The weather was often given as the reason why his customers had to hold off paying their fuel bills. As a result, my family suffered with the weather along with everyone else. I never heard my father get persistent with any of his customers, even if they had bills running back over several years. He took all sorts of items as partial settlement of outstanding bills. I remember the day he arrived home with a used vacuum cleaner and my mother berated him because there was absolutely no way that we needed two vacuums. Having grown up on a farm himself, my father understood the farmer's precarious life. Mother also grew up on a farm, but she didn't have his empathy. Some of his customers were appreciative of his understanding of their plight and remained loyal customers for many years.

In winter the ice storms left the countryside a frozen wonderland. My father told me of being able to ice skate to school down the frozen dirt roads near his parents' farm west of Sedan. He broke his nose by hitting a clod sticking up through the ice on one of those dirt roads. His nose resembled that of a boxer for the rest of his life. I remember being able to climb on the frozen drifts to the roofs of the sheds at the back of our house.

The frequent ice and snow storms made the main street of Cedar Vale impassible several times each winter. Town officials blocked off the main (Cedar) street from the bank building on Highway 166 all the way up to the water tower at the top of the hill. The entire area became our sledding hill, and we could get up tremendous speed coming down the hill. The long walk back up to the water tower was strenuous but well worth it for the thrill of the ride back down. The speed could be dangerous, however, since it was sometimes a challenge to get stopped before we crossed Highway 166. I remember at least one major injury, a fellow student who lost a kidney in a sledding accident on one of the hills in town.

In summer there were nearly nightly tornado watches or warnings. Those more faint-hearted souls would "go to the cellar" at the first sign of storm clouds. Since we lived in town and didn't have a cellar, or even a basement, we just weathered the storms. I thought of us as being very brave in the face of those monsters. Since we had nowhere to go, I became quite accustomed to watching storms gather, dump rain, wind, and sometimes hail, and pass over. I remember watching trees and power lines go down, hail storms that left our yard filled with drifts of ice, and twisters that passed us by. The most terrifying storm I remember was the tornado that passed over Cedar Vale on its way to devastating Udall, Kansas; when it touched down, it left not a single house in the town intact. People from Cedar Vale went to Udall to help out with the cleanup and returned with stories of horrific devastation.

Another frequent occurrence was the flooding of nearby rivers and streams. There was an area between Sedan and Caney that was often under water after heavy rains. Since we had relatives living near Caney, we sometimes had to travel on Highway 166 during this flooding. I remember my father driving onto a stretch of road just east of Niotaze that was covered with swirling water. He had to drive very slowly lest the water get into the engine compartment and flood out the engine. Mother was terrified and softly cursed him all the way to the other side for risking our lives. In later years that stretch of road was built up several feet, and the constant flooding became a thing of the past.

Cedar Vale is also prone to flooding of the Caney River and the surrounding creeks, and I remember looking out at a swirling, muddy sea filling the area just east of town. We took all this as a matter of course and adjusted our lives accordingly.

I think the turbulent Kansas weather was a significant factor in the development of our stoic, persistent characters. We learned to take adversity without complaint and to enjoy what nature put in our paths with good, if somewhat fatalistic, humor.

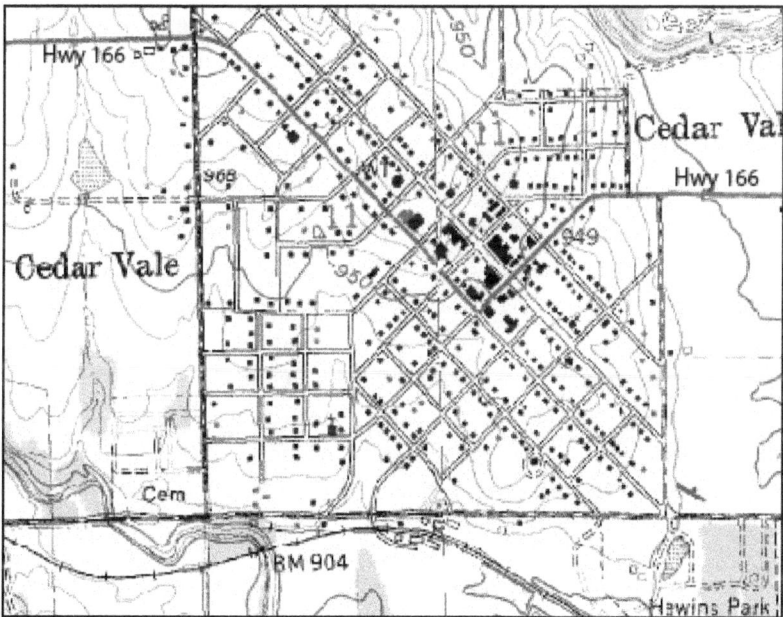

Map of Cedar Vale in the 1950s.

Free Enterprise

As youngsters growing up in Cedar Vale, Kansas, my friends and I were indoctrinated into the capitalist system at an early age. We were, in short, good young Americans. We understood the advantages of buying at wholesale and selling at retail to make a profit, and we were anxious to enter into the wonderful world of sales.

When I was eight years old we were living in a house on Highway 166, on the southwest corner across from the telephone office where my mother worked. The high school was diagonally across the street and a larger, stone house occupied the other corner. That house was later occupied by Mrs. Morris, the vocal instructor at the school, but that was many years later. There was an open lot on the south next to our house, where my father planted a big vegetable garden. At the back was a tool shed that was mostly used as the kids' playhouse. Across the alley was the Thatcher house, where my friends and playmates Donna and Jim lived. Donna was a year older than me and Jim was several years younger.

The first commercial venture I remember was a company I formed at age eight with Donna and Jim. The Thatchers' mother planted a large flower garden every summer, and my father had a large vegetable garden. Late in the summer Donna, Jim, and I harvested hollyhock and morning glory seeds from the Thatcher garden and green and lima beans from my father's garden, and we set up our seed company. To add to our stock, I had found a number of booklets called *Dawn to Dusk on the Farm*, which my father would give out to his farm customers as he traveled around the countryside selling gasoline and oil. These books were clearly marked "Compliments of your Standard Oil agent," but that didn't deter me in the slightest. The booklets were a treasure trove of practical information useful to farmers and their wives, and they proved best sellers for our budding seed business. We loaded all this stuff in a wagon and walked around the neighborhood selling door to door. This business went bust when my father found out that we were selling his "free" booklets and forced us to return all the money we had earned.

Undeterred by this initial business failure, our next venture was the fur business. The Thatchers maintained two or three rabbit hutches. They butchered the large white bunnies for meat. That gave us a ready supply of rabbit pelts. We hit upon the idea of nailing them up inside the shed at the back of my house to dry out. We thought that we would probably be able to sell the pelts, since there actually was a fur business not more than a block from our houses. This second business failed when the odor from the shed attracted the attention of my mother, who cleaned out the mess and thoroughly fumigated the place.

Most of my early businesses were totally legal, but once I did stray into an extortion scheme. This event took place several years later, when I was a teenager living in the western part of Cedar Vale. Jim's older sister, Donna, and her friends, Pat and Janice, had taken photos of each other at a slumber party. These were "cheesecake" photos that showed a lot of arm and shoulder and just a hint of cleavage. They had printed the names of their current boyfriends on their shoulders in lipstick. Somehow Jim obtained the negatives (perhaps by pilfering from his sister's bedroom). He presented them to me since I had a photo darkroom in a closet in my house, and we hatched our plot. We printed several copies of each of the photos and began distributing them to the girls, hoping for some profit or perhaps just to get a rise out of them. The girls were totally outraged that we had these suggestive photos and ratted to our parents. Both Jim and I were severely punished. That put an end to my short life of crime.

All this free-enterprise training served me well as I grew older. In my early teens I sold subscriptions to *Grit* magazine from door to door, actually making a profit. Later, I obtained a catalog containing all sorts of household articles. I could sell these items at retail and then order from the company at wholesale and make a nice profit. In later years, my door-to-door training served me well when there were school or church sales of magazine subscriptions, candy bars, and the like. I had already learned how to knock on doors and present an attractive sales spiel, so I was well prepared to pursue the great American dream of financial independence and a well-paying job.

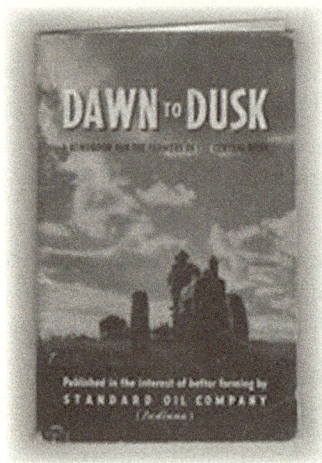

DAWN to DUSK

Published in the interest of better farming by
STANDARD OIL COMPANY
(Indiana)

Listening to Jazz on a Saturday Night

When I was in early adolescence my interest in music become all-consuming. I played and sang and listened as much as I could to all kinds of music that was available to me. This mostly consisted of country-and-western bands (Bob Wills and His Texas Playboys) and my school ensembles (band and chorus) for live music, and the recordings that I heard on the jukeboxes and over the radio. It was only when I went away to summer music camp at the University of Kansas as a high-school junior that I heard a live symphony orchestra, and I thought it was the most wonderful thing imaginable. Immediately I said that one day I would compose music for symphony orchestra.

I don't know quite how it happened, but I chanced on a late-night radio broadcast from New Orleans that came in only on Saturday nights. There was a half-hour show that was broadcast live from a ballroom "high atop" one of the hotels in downtown New Orleans, followed by a recorded history of jazz program on the same station. The music was all Dixieland, and it was the authentic stuff, a far cry from the sanitized versions I had heard on recordings. I was hooked completely, and every Saturday night I listened to this broadcast. I can't remember exactly why, but for some reason I listened on the car radio in my parents' old Plymouth parked in front of our house. Perhaps it was because my parents needed to get their sleep, or perhaps they didn't approve of my taste in music, but I always chose the car as a listening place. To this day, whenever I hear Dixieland I see the glow of the car radio in that old Plymouth and the dark house in front of me. The gritty sounds of Dixieland mingled with the song of cicadas on long summer nights, and the scratchy old recordings on the history program only added to the atmosphere. I tried to imagine what it would be like to be in the glamorous city of New Orleans where, I was told, this music was played around the clock. I imitated the style, as best I could, on my trumpet, and spent hours playing variations on "Saints" and "South Rampart Street Parade."

Imagine my surprise when I learned that this music, which I loved, had been invented and was mostly played by people with black skins. I had had no direct contact with "Negroes" (that was the polite name we had for African-Americans at that time, but all my relatives used the more common name that would shock all of us today if we heard it). In Cedar Vale, Kansas, black people were, by city ordinance, not allowed to remain in town after the sun went down. If any blacks came to town at night they were escorted to the city limits by the town marshal. The neighboring town, Sedan, did have a Negro section, which my relatives called "Darkytown." I had seen black people on the street but had never so much as spoken to one of them. To think that these people, whom everyone laughed about and called lazy and stupid, had somehow created that beautiful, vivid music was beyond my comprehension. This revelation made me mistrust the judgment of those who had called blacks stupid. I had evidence to the contrary that was irrefutable.

Quite unknown to the Cedar Vale city marshal, black people had been visiting our little town every Saturday night for a long time, and he had totally missed them! What a dereliction of duty! Even now, I have to smile when I think about that. What irony that this white boy was sneaking out at night to absorb the most unique musical art form that Americans have created—an art form invented and played by people who couldn't even stay overnight in our Hotel Roosevelt. Sweet it would be if I didn't feel shame and guilt over that evil part of our nation's history. That painful history must have been the source of the cutting anger that I sensed and responded to in even the most rousing, upbeat rendition of "South Rampart Street Parade."

From the perspective of the recent devastation of New Orleans and our government's poor response to it, I am sorry to say that not enough has changed in race relations in our country except for a polite covering of political correctness. Of course, city ordinances like the one in place in Cedar Vale in the 1940s would not be constitutional now—if they were then. I do sense that Madison Avenue has awakened to the fact that African-Americans are a significant economic force in our economy. There are nearly always people of color in every television commercial and in all magazine advertising. And politicians are acutely aware that racial minorities do vote. Change comes slowly, but change it will.

Bertha Kirby

My spiritual development as a child was intimately bound up with music. I first discovered my love of music by singing with my parents. We sang together nearly every day as soon as I could speak, and singing was our principal entertainment when we were driving anywhere. When I was nine years old I asked for a piano and piano lessons. I will never forget the huge old upright piano being delivered to my room. It nearly filled all the available space. I could actually reach the keyboard from my bed.

I remember playing on the keyboard very softly late at night so I wouldn't wake my parents. I spent a lot of time exploring the piano, even before the lessons began. It was with the beginning of piano lessons that I first came to know Mrs. Kirby.

Bertha Kirby was the widow of a prominent local doctor. She was one of the two piano teachers in Cedar Vale at the time. She was quite elderly, with hands deformed by arthritis, so playing was no longer easy for her. Nevertheless, she traveled around town in her 1930 black Chevy coupe giving lessons in people's homes.

It seems that Dr. Kirby had lost his wife at a young age, leaving him to raise twin baby daughters. The story that was told around Cedar Vale was that Bertha was a "mail order" bride, but my research shows that she was the daughter of William and Sarah McNeely, who moved to Cedar Vale from Missouri early in the twentieth century. Dr. Kirby must have known Bertha (or Bessie, as she was called before marriage) in Chautauqua County. All this occurred many years before

I knew her. I remember being in her home several times; the living room table was completely covered with copies of *Etude* magazine, the magazine for piano teachers. She was a devoted piano teacher and a prominent citizen of the town.

The peculiarities of Mrs. Kirby's driving were well known around Cedar Vale, and everyone knew to watch out for her. Mrs. Kirby would look up and down the street very carefully before getting into her car, but once in her Chevy coupe, she never looked to the right or left—assuming, perhaps, that the traffic conditions would not have changed much in the minute or so since she had last checked. Mrs. Kirby seldom shifted out of first gear, so we got used to hearing her old car screaming along up the road.

Mrs. Kirby would arrive at my home at the appointed time even in the worst weather. I remember my mother giving her something warm to drink to thaw her out in the middle of the winter, and saying that she should not have tried to make it. However, neither rain nor hail could deter Mrs. Kirby from her appointed rounds.

If a student showed particular promise, Mrs. Kirby would appear again in the middle of the week to "help you with your practice." I had the equivalent of two lessons per week for several years. For all this personal attention, Mrs. Kirby charged twenty-five cents per week. We wondered how Mrs. Kirby was able to support herself on piano lessons alone; in truth, she probably couldn't. An inheritance from her husband must have made up the difference.

Mrs. Kirby was a strict and demanding teacher. I remember many times when she rapped me across the knuckles with a pencil when I missed a note. If things were going well with a piece, her quiet "one, two" counting might fade out as she dozed off, but the slightest miscue would jar her into full consciousness, and the pencil would lash out. Far from being an ogre, Mrs. Kirby was lavish in her praise of good work. She was also the first person who recognized my creative abilities.

I have often said that my original inspiration as a composer was John Thompson's beginning piano book, *Teaching Little Fingers to Play*. I realized right away that I could write more interesting music than any piece in that book! In fact, I did write a piece each week for Mrs. Kirby. I don't recall her asking me to do so, but she was clearly pleased and impressed that I did. She told my mother that I had creative talent and might some day be a composer. I wish that some of my early pieces had been saved, but all were lost at some point.

After about three years of study with Mrs. Kirby, I started trumpet lessons and stopped studying piano. The thought of playing in the school band was seductive. The piano, by comparison, seemed a solitary pursuit. I have lived to regret that choice since I later had no need to play the trumpet, but I used the piano every day in my teaching and composing. Even when I was no longer her student, Mrs. Kirby continued to follow my musical development and was always complementary of my efforts.

Religious Education

My contact with religion while I was growing up in Cedar Vale could best be described as "shopping around." I was not encouraged or discouraged from church attendance by my parents. I would not describe them as atheists or even agnostics, they were just not interested in church attendance. I never knew of my grandparents attending church. My grandfather Call was what I would call an active agnostic and a humanist. My parents, on the other hand, simply thought that churches were social institutions where people seemed to fight as often as pray.

I was very interested in religion from the time I was eight or nine years of age (see "Going to Sunday School for the First Time," p. 24). I periodically attended Sunday school at both the Methodist church and the Baptist church in Cedar Vale. I went to Vacation Bible School at the local Assembly of God Church, which was not far from my home, and, at least once, went to the Baptist Bible School. When I was older I was a regular member of the Baptist Youth Fellowship (BYF) and actually was baptized in that church sometime during my high school years.

I was interested in the Bible and, at one point when I was ten or eleven, started to copy the entire King James Bible on a scroll, so it would be more like I imagined the original might have been. I didn't make it very far into Genesis before the size of that task overwhelmed me. The unfinished scroll remained in my bedroom for years thereafter.

I participated in the other Protestant churches in Cedar Vale to a lesser extent. I remember being invited to activities at the Church of Christ, perhaps by Marilyn Holroyd, who was a good friend of mine. I knew that there were also a Catholic church and an Episcopal church in the town, but they seemed to be little attended. The buildings always struck me as nearly abandoned, even though they were kept up as well as the other churches.

My "shopping" among the churches was more a matter of which of my friends went there than any theological consideration. I enjoyed singing and liked to sing the hymns when I attended church services. I was far from a regular church attender, but I did attend services at all the protestant churches in town.

When I went away to college I pretty much left the churches behind, except for the times I visited my parents. They had moved to Minneapolis, Kansas, the summer after my high-school graduation and bought a house next door to the local Baptist church. The minister at that church was a cornet player, and I arranged duets for us to play at church when I was home from college. It was at his suggestion that I began to date a young member of that church. She became my first wife. We were married in a country Methodist church near her father's farm.

Religion was always a matter of personal choice for me and I gradually moved away from any church affiliation. When I was teaching in the public schools in Dolores, Colorado, I made great friends with the local Methodist minister and did attend his church regularly (see "Climbing a 14er," p. 77). His religious views were very liberal and humanist, and I felt right at home in his church. It was only when my own children came along that I began to consider their religious education. That brought me to the Unitarian Universalist Fellowship in Ames, Iowa, where I found a congenial church home for the years when my children were growing up. It was in that fellowship that I met the love of my life, Elyn. She was a lifelong member of the Unitarian Fellowship, which her parents had helped to found. We attended the fellowship until we moved to Denver, Colorado, where Elyn was studying to become a Unitarian Universalist minister. While in Denver we attended the Universalist church that Elyn served, along with periodic visits to other churches that Elyn was interested in.

For the majority of my life I described myself as an agnostic, like my grandfather Call, but I have gradually come to see more and more that is not explainable using my five senses or science. I have come to embrace the "mystery" and am seeking to work with it in every way I can. Retreats, meditation practices, and body work have all opened me up to a deeper appreciation of the realm of spirit. Organized religion, to me, is still much more about human power and control—not spirit—in spite of all protests to the contrary. I would describe myself as a spiritual person, but not as a religious person.

A House, But Not a Home

As I look back over my twenty-eight-year-long life as a university professor I see a pattern that I was not aware of as I was living it. I seemed to always be on my way to somewhere else. There were weeks and months that I lived in isolation in various places while writing major compositions. I found it difficult to sustain the concentration required to produce large-scale works unless I could be totally isolated and work around the clock. At various times I spent blocks of time in south Texas, rural Iowa, and other places where I would rent a cabin or apartment for a short time.

My first wife and I seemed to be the proverbial ships passing in the night for most of our time together. There were the years when she lived away from home while she was in law school. There was the pattern we established after we had children of taking separate vacations. That allowed the children to have a full-time parent at home. We took our parenting responsibilities very seriously but for some reason thought only one parent was necessary at any given time to discharge those responsibilities. Maybe it was easier that way. If the demands of our schedules didn't allow either of us to be at home we hired help. From time to time we had people living in the house to help out with child care. That was particularly necessary when one of us was living elsewhere.

These were the years when the concept of "open marriage" was exploding into popular culture. I embraced the concept wholeheartedly and engaged in relationships outside my marriage. These were handled openly, without deceit, and I prided myself on being very sensible about such matters. For me, those relationships were often the only opportunities I had to enjoy the intimacy that was missing at home. The patterns that came out of my early life in Cedar Vale seemed to make it impossible for me to sustain a relationship with one person without periodic escape. It would be easy to say that I had a desire for sexual variety, but it goes much deeper than that.

When we could afford it, my wife purchased a small cabin in rural Iowa. This gave me a place to do my composing that didn't require extensive travel and the expense of renting accommodations. It also was a place where she could go to be alone or to be with someone else. I would sometimes take the children to the cabin to live while my wife was traveling or busy at home, and she would do the same.

Handling our schedule was like planning a railroad timetable. All the destination points and times would be put on the table and a plan developed for accomplishing the schedule. It all worked beautifully. We never neglected the children and we got most of what we wanted. In many ways I'm sure that our pattern didn't look much different from many busy families. The part that was different was the part that didn't show from the outside—there was really no center at the center.

The pattern I see as I look back is of two people on their way to somewhere, but seldom was the destination the same for both. Another way of looking at this pattern is that we were both moving away from each other as much as we were moving toward something else.

In recognizing this I take full responsibility for my part in creating that empty center. It "takes two to tango" and I was certainly doing my part. It may well be that I did more than my part for this failure at the center, but I don't have enough clarity yet to be certain.

Perhaps that clarity will come. I have been working very hard these past years to gain as much clarity as possible and I can see some progress. I don't expect to come to a place where the whole pattern of my life emerges. The best I can do is sift through all these pebbles, these little scenes and vignettes. By careful examination of each I hope to see the events of my life more clearly than while I was experiencing them.

One thing I marvel at as I look back is how I managed to do all I did. It seems like it would take at least two lifetimes or a clone of myself to do it all. Perhaps there is some truth to my birth sign—Gemini, the twins. Those who believe in astrology would certainly agree.

Body Work

One way that I kept myself together during the most grueling years when I was a college professor/textbook author/composer/book designer was to have regular massages. When I first went to a massage therapist, she would ask me, "So, how does your body feel today?" And I would reply, "Body, what body?" I was so completely wrapped up in my head that I couldn't even feel my body unless something was hurting. That gradually changed as I had a massage every week.

An extension of this growing body awareness came after I left my first marriage and was striking out in all sorts of new directions. One direction I tried and liked a lot were workshops sponsored by Body Electric School in the Bay Area of California. The name, "Body Electric" came from the Walt Whitman poem "I sing the body electric . . ." Body Electric School was started during the AIDS epidemic in the Bay Area. A group of gay men got together to teach other gay men how to have an erotic life without spreading HIV. That efforts like this were successful is proven by the drastic decrease in new HIV cases among the gay population in the Bay Area. By the time I was doing this work, it had expanded to include workshops for straight men, women, and workshops for women and men together, along with a massage-therapy school leading to certification in California. Body Electric workshops are billed as "Erotic adventures for the soul," and there is certainly a deep spiritual content in these workshops. To say that these are "clothes off" events may give you the picture of orgies, but the workshops are far from uncontrolled excess. In fact, they are well planned, progressive experiences of deep body awareness unlike anything I have experienced anywhere else.

At one of these workshops one of the leaders was talking about how one could be a "useful" person in one's community by giving of one's talents and skills. The idea of being a useful person made a positive impression on me. When I looked at my talents and skills, the first thing that came to mind was to learn massage. I had noticed that I have what are called "good hands" that can feel and sense the state of muscles below the skin and work with them. I had been in great demand within the Body Electric workshops for my natural massage skills. I came home from that workshop and relayed this to my beloved Elyn, who said, "Do it." It happened that Body Electric had a massage school training starting the following week. I applied, was accepted, and in just a few days found myself in Oakland, California, as a massage school student. I took to the training like the proverbial duck to water and very soon was a certified massage therapist. I opted not to be licensed in the State of Colorado where we were living at the time because I intended to never charge a fee for my services, and I never have.

After several years of doing massage for friends I took classes at a local Boulder massage school called Phenomenal Touch Institute. The founder of this school had been my massage therapist for over a year. I liked her techniques and wanted to include them in my own work. After studying Phenomenal Touch for a year or so I was asked to become an assistant in teaching her work. I assisted in the training of Phenomenal Touch students for over a year before we left Boulder, Colorado, to relocate to Santa Fe, New Mexico.

Giving massage is very healing for me. I like being in contact with bodies and I find that I always feel better myself when I finish working on someone. It is very much as if we are both getting a massage at the same time. I also feel that I'm being a "useful" person for my clients, which is deeply satisfying for me.

It is my intention to offer massage to friends when they want the work and when we are well attuned to each other. This means that there are times when I'm doing more than one session per week and weeks when I do none. This is just fine with me since I have no ambition to go into business. As I say to my friends, "I have already had several careers in my life and I don't intend to have another."

Mr. Beggs and the High School Band

In the sixth grade I started trumpet lessons with Mr. Beggs, the band director of the Cedar Vale schools. Mr. Beggs was himself an excellent cornet player, and I tried very hard to live up to the high standards he set for himself and his students. I remember my early lessons were a struggle for me. I was trying so hard to get everything right; more than once I broke into tears when I couldn't perform up to our mutual expectations. Mr. Beggs was always kind, but a bit cool. He answered my frustrations by telling me that I would be able to do it if I would just practice more each day.

Somewhere in my second year of study, I must have had a breakthrough, because I can remember Mr. Beggs asking me to join the high-school band. I was in the seventh grade at the time, but Mr. Beggs would pick me up at the grade school and drive me to the high school for the rehearsal. There were two or three other grade school students who were given similar treatment, but I felt very special because I was the youngest. I thought that playing in the high-school band and having my own band uniform was the most exciting thing that had ever happened to me. Now that I look back on it, I'm sure that Mr. Beggs simply needed to fill out the trumpet section, but at the time I was sure that it was because of my superior musical ability.

I redoubled my efforts and practiced the trumpet every available minute after school, trying to reach the level of the high school players. Don Schaffer, who was three years older and already sitting first chair in the trumpet section, particularly inspired me. Don could play the most demanding solos, higher and faster than anything I had ever heard. He was at least as good as Mr. Beggs himself. I gradually worked my way up in the section over the next few years, so that when Don graduated and began studying music at the University of Kansas, I took his place as the first chair in the trumpet section.

Mr. Beggs always showed his appreciation for my effort, but he kept my ego in check by finding some more challenging solo for me to master. And, of course, there was always Don Schaffer, who came home from college playing circles around me. Mr. Beggs encouraged me to play by ear as well as performing from printed music. He was a member of a local dance band and an accomplished improviser on the cornet. In the last year or so of high school he occasionally invited me to join him on the bandstand at local dances, and we shared the solos. This experience of playing by ear was excellent training and a good starting point for later compositional work. The most important lesson that I learned from Mr. Beggs was that I would have to set very high standards for myself to be successful in music. I sensed that he had to work very hard to meet his own professional standards, and I tried to emulate him as best I could.

It was because of him that I chose a career in music, and I certainly owe him a debt for instilling high personal standards, which were indeed necessary for success in the music profession. Mr. Beggs went on from Cedar Vale to direct bands in larger school systems. He devoted his entire life to the public-school band. In 1980, when I learned that Mr. Beggs was retiring after nearly forty years of teaching, I wrote a piece for band and dedicated it to him. This work, called *Homage*, became my first published composition for band, and it was a proud moment for me to be able to send Mr. Beggs a copy of the published score.

Bullies

Cedar Vale, Kansas, had an elementary school for grades one through eight and a high school for grades nine through twelve. During my elementary school years I had to deal with bullies nearly all the time. The abuse began in the early grades and increased in intensity for the rest of elementary school. In my experience I don't remember teachers intervening to break up playground fights among the boys in the school. Only one teacher was usually assigned to each of the three playgrounds, and that teacher just stood by and watched without taking any action.

The student body was very sharply divided between the "town" kids and the "country" kids. There was considerable resentment between the two groups, and in later years a group of the country kids formed a gang that terrorized the townies. The country kids were generally stronger and rougher than the townies since they were doing farm labor at home. They seemed to be ahead in physical development and somewhat behind in intellectual development as a general rule. In retrospect, I can see that the group who formed the gang were boys who found school work very difficult to do. They must have resented those of us who sailed through our lessons and always got the good grades while they were left struggling in a system where they could never catch up and were falling farther behind all the time.

I was even more a target for abuse since I had no inclination for rough-and-tumble play and preferred music, art, and reading. In short, I was a sissy in their eyes. Sex-role stereotyping was never questioned in those days as it is today. However, even in these enlightened times, the Hollywood action star who has been playing the part of "Governor of California" can still refer to "girly men" and get by with it. "The more things change . . ."

My mother was extremely over-protective and would not allow me to go out for sports lest I injure myself. That only contributed to me being seen as a "girly boy." Of course, my mother was absolutely correct that organized sports are a great source of injuries that often lead to disabilities later in life. As I renew contact these days with my high-school graduating classmates, who are in their 70s, I hear stories of knee replacements, hip replacements, and shoulders and arms that cause constant pain, all the result of organized sports in high school.

Recess time was always a time of greatest danger for me. I tried to avoid the bullies as best I could and would often stand with my back to the school wall so no one could get to me from behind. Even so, I was often caught out and beaten up by the gang. Even more frightening was the verbal abuse that these boys put out. I can well remember a day when I was in the eighth grade when one of the gang members showed me his pocket knife and calmly informed me that they intended to castrate me at the next recess. I spent that day in complete terror and tried unsuccessfully to stay inside the school house at recess. Of course, nothing happened and I'm sure that the teacher assigned to the playground would have intervened if they had really tried to make good on their promise.

For me, the move to high school was a godsend. The gang broke up or went into shop and vocational-agriculture classes, and I became somewhat of a "star" in the music department. My contact with that group was also minimized because I was taking the "college prep" classes that they couldn't make it through.

Returning to Cedar Vale for my thirtieth class reunion I was amazed to see how those boys had aged as adults. I was at the peak of my career and I could see that they were beyond their peak and already becoming old men. That dissolved any lingering dislike I might have still felt for them. And I can now say, "Well, governor Arnold, there are worse things than being a girly man."

Altered States

In the early 1970s, when I was actively pursuing the so-called "hippy" counter-culture lifestyle in my spare time, I traveled in circles where there was considerable drug use. Since the bulk of my time was devoted to being a professor and moving up in the academic ranks, this was only a pursuit that occupied some vacations and breaks in the academic calendar. I was only a part-time hippy!

I saw the use of most of the soft drugs that were then popular, such as pot, acid, and mushrooms. I never tried LSD, but I did experiment with pot and mushrooms. While I found the experience very pleasant, I noticed that I always felt a certain "fuzziness" afterwards that would last for several days. I noticed that people who were regular users seemed always to be slightly unfocused. I realized very quickly that in my other life I couldn't accomplish what I wanted to accomplish without total focus and concentration, so I decided against the use of any drugs, including alcohol for the most part. I have no regrets for having made that decision.

Non-drug-induced altered states were quite another matter. Early in my professional career I experimented with self-hypnosis as an aid to composing (see "Composing II," p. 95), and I tried various meditation techniques over the years. While not being as quick and powerful as taking drugs, meditation, if practiced regularly, brings about altered states that are life-changing, pleasant, and produce no hangover. From time to time I practiced Rebirthing™, Holotrophic™ breath work, yoga, Tai Chi, Healing Touch™, and a variety of Sufi and Hindu practices.

It was during the time in 1993, when I was leaving my first marriage (see "Days of Reckoning," p. 28), that I became very actively involved with Sufi and Hindu practice. I attended a *satsang* most Friday evenings. These evenings were devoted to chanting and prayers to the various Hindu deities. The effect of an evening of sustained chanting was to put me into a very different mental space, a space where I gained a sense of timelessness and saw the everyday world for what it is, just a mental construct that we all agree upon. In that space, there is always peace and equanimity. As an alternative to the emotional meat grinder I was going through with the divorce, it was a welcome change of pace. It was at these *satsang* evenings that I first made significant contact with my second wife-to-be, Elyn.

A woman, Bonnie R., in the Unitarian Fellowship in Ames would sometimes offer classes in Sufi practices and I took several of these. This led to my initiation into the Sufi Order International and doing regular individual spiritual practices suggested by Bonnie. I actively did Sufi practices for over ten years and did several intensive individual silent retreats with the Sufi Order (see "A Healing," p. 52). The Sufi practices sustained me and gave me a deeper understanding of myself and my relationship with others and the world than I had had before. I left the Sufi Order in 2006 when I became disenchanted with the subtle patriarchy I found there. Since that time I have been working with a teacher in the Western Esoteric Traditions named R. J. Stewart. I find a refreshing gender balance in this work, and it is very satisfying to come in contact with spiritual traditions that come out of Europe instead of Asia or the Middle East. Since my own cultural heritage is European this work seems to be a good fit.

I would call my regular spiritual practice my most important task at this stage of my life. As I approach the end of this lifetime I feel a sense of peace with the process of growing older and I look forward to the next adventures that will unfold, both while I'm living and when I move on to other planes.

Railroad Memories

We are driving south down Highway 285 through Colorado back home to Santa Fe. Near the New Mexico border, Highway 285 crosses the tracks of the Cumbres & Toltec Scenic Railway, a narrow-gauge rail line that meanders through some amazing mountain country along the Colorado/New Mexico border. Just as we come up to the station an old coal-burning steam engine crosses in front of us pushing three cars of gravel to be used to maintain the track ahead.

Suddenly I am back in Cedar Vale at the train station on the south edge of town, where the Missouri Pacific Railway connects Cedar Vale with points east and west. I am about seven years of age and my mother and I are waiting to take the train from Cedar Vale to Sedan. My father needs to pick up some oil or other products from Leo Chrisman, the Standard Oil agent in Sedan. As a lark, he leaves Mother and me off at the MOPAC station, where we purchase tickets from the station agent, our neighbor, Dewey Burch. We are going to have a train ride to Sedan, where Dad will pick us up and drive us back the Cedar Vale. I can hardly contain my excitement when that huge black engine roars into the station and we board the only passenger car. The passenger car is just like you see in the old Western movies. There are ancient steel seats covered with worn and cracked leather. At the end of the car is a primitive toilet and a water bottle and small cone-shaped cups that you can pull from a dispenser and get a drink. Of course, I will need to use the toilet and get a drink of that railroad water! That is just part of the excitement of the journey. All the windows are open because it is summer and, of course, the compartment is not air conditioned.

Are Frank and Jesse James or the Dalton boys out there waiting to hold up the train? Will we be attacked by Indians in full war paint? My imagination is running wild as we pull out of the station and begin to cross through territory that is totally unfamiliar to me. I have seen all the roads around western Chautauqua County, but the railroad passes through areas where there are no roads. Out across wooded areas, through deep cuts into the hills, and alongside farms and ranches we go, and it is all just as I imagined it would be, except for the robbers and Indian attacks.

A continuous rain of coal soot pours into the windows and greatly distresses my mother, who is the soul of fastidiousness. But all this is just part of the thrill for me, and I don't mind my clothes getting covered with small black specks. Mother tries in vain to brush them off and that just spreads them out, making the spots bigger.

All too soon we pull into the Sedan railway station and there is Dad with his big red tank-wagon truck waiting for us. What stories I have to tell and tell them I do, with eyes wide with excitement from the adventure we just had. Dad laughs as I tell my stories while Mother fumes a bit at the black spots on our clothes.

This scene from my childhood rolls in front of my eyes as I wait the few minutes for the Cumbres & Toltec Scenic Railway engine to push those cars past us and clear the tracks for our continued journey. Very soon we will be in home country, where the place names suddenly are all in Spanish—Rio Arriba, Tres Piedras, Ojo Caliente. Now I know we are nearly home.

The Cumbres & Toltec Scenic Railway

Music and Technology I

Cedar Vale

"To the musician who should be an engineer." wrote our CVHS science teacher, Mr. Williams. That statement nicely encapsulates the twin interests that have been with me throughout life. As a youngster I was an avid reader of *Science Digest*, a smallish magazine that reported the latest wonders of science and technology. I remember reading an article in the early 1950s about how "electronic brains" would someday make work obsolete. That really appealed to me, being the lazy boy I was. I imagined a world where all of us were on permanent vacation, visiting south sea islands and lying on the beach drinking rum and coke. (More exotic drinks were beyond my imagination at the time.) It is ironic that now we are all slaves to our computers and far from making work obsolete, Americans now work more hours per week on average than they did in the 1950s. So much for the value of prediction.

When my interests veered toward chemistry I memorized all the abbreviations for the elements and studied how they were combined in my own home chemistry lab, creating horrible, stinky messes in the process. No old alarm clock was safe from my prying fingers. I took several apart and put them back together many times, which didn't improve their ability to keep accurate time. I built my own multi-band radio with some help from Glen Toothacker, the radio repairman at L.

C. Adam Mercantile, and it actually worked. I would monitor the police and aircraft communications bands waiting for snatches of voice communications among all the Morse code transmissions from ham radio operators that were more prevalent in those days. And, yes, I did try to learn Morse code, but the transmissions were always too fast for me to understand.

You may have noticed that the passions I was pursuing were all "extracurricular." In high-school science classes I usually already had enough knowledge to get by without study. This earned me the epitaph, "Why study when my brilliant questions baffle the instructors," beside my picture in the senior yearbook. I was satisfied with my B or B+, leaving the A grades for Wayne Woodruff and Reva Ramey.

In fact, I went through CVHS mostly as an extracurricular student: music, girls, science, and technology. Many years later, when my son was a senior in high school, I was called in by his math teacher, who told me that Greg was making a C grade in calculus while, at the same time, he had just scored above the 99th percentile in math on his SATs (see Raising Kids, p. 20). How could I discipline a son to do ALL the problems when I would likely have acted exactly the same way when I was his age?

Greg is a highly successful engineer, so Mr. Williams' predictions that I should have taken that as my occupation have now come true in a second generation.

Music and Technology II

Undergraduate Years

When I became a student at the University of Kansas it was as a music education major. The deal I made with my parents for majoring in such an impractical area as music was that I would take a degree where I could get a job after four years. The Mus. Ed. degree would allow me to teach in the public schools. Once at the university my interests quickly shifted toward composition and I declared myself a double major. My interest in science and technology seemed to have faded into the background, but the composition major was just another expression of it. The composer is a programmer who writes a program in an esoteric code called music notation, and the performers are the computers who realize the composer's program (although performers add their own personal stamp on the music, unlike a computer).

I was finding less and less interest in the performing areas, in spite of the fact that I was advised that I could have a career as an opera singer if I would give up all my various interests and concentrate on training my voice. By that time, the lure of being a composer had already taken hold and I had to keep my Mus. Ed. degree going for the sake of my parents. There simply wasn't time, or inclination, to give it all up for opera.

To pursue a double major and finish in four years would require enrolling in summer school. I financed summer session by hiring on as a dorm counsellor at Midwestern Music and Art Camp and taking a part-time job with the Registrar's office at the university. I was assigned to the transcript department, where I quickly developed a skill that made me a very attractive employee. The transcripts were printed using a photostatic process. This was in the days before photocopy machines and laser printers. A huge "Rube Goldberg" of a machine approximately 6 feet by 5 feet by 10 feet in the back of the Registrar's office produced the photostats. These were reverse (black became white and white became black) images of the hand-written permanent records that were stored in dark basement areas of Strong Hall. My early training in taking alarm clocks apart and reassembling them came to my aid in this job. I quickly learned how to keep that tempermental beast of a machine that combined a photo enlarger with a wet-process photo-developing and drying process in operation. I was able to save the office from most of the frequent calls for repair that had plagued them up to that time. I understood photo processing because I had a small photo darkroom in a closet off my bedroom in Cedar Vale. I soon had a job where I could work as many hours as I wanted both summer and winter.

I was on the staff at the Registrar's office when the first 914 Xerox copier was installed and the photostat machine was phased out. The 914, so named because it would print on plain paper up to 9 inches by 14 inches (legal size with 1/2 inch margin to spare), was a most wonderful innovation. Suddenly transcripts could be produced in a few seconds, and the result looked very much like the original black on white permanent records. As the resident "techie" I was assigned the task of getting the new machine up and running and figuring out how to produce transcripts on it. So, while I was pursuing high art in my life as a student, I was making a living as a technologist for the Registrar. The twin interests continued.

Music and Technology III

KU Graduate Student Years

When I finished my Mus. Ed. degree from the University of Kansas I was still about one year away from a degree in music composition. I took a year off at that point to teach in the Hoxie, Kansas, public schools and then returned to KU to finish the B. Mus. in composition. At the end of that year I was offered a two-year graduate assistantship teaching music theory to first- and second-year music students while completing a Master of Music degree in composition. Now I had an office, a regular schedule as a teacher, and a new wife. It was during those two years that I really began to flourish as a composer.

One day I looked out of my office window in the music building and saw a delivery truck backed up to the adjoining business school building. Seeing pieces of high tech equipment being unloaded, I decided to investigate. Sure enough, an IBM 650 digital computer was being installed in the building next door. This was not the first computer on the KU campus. The administrative offices in Strong Hall had a computer, and the university was in the process of making registration and other record keeping computer-assisted. However, this new IBM 650 was for student use, and one could sign up for a short course of three or four classes and then be allowed to program and operate the computer. There was a sign-up sheet in the computer room, and when your time arrived the computer was yours for an hour. I immediately signed up for the short course and took my turn operating the computer.

This brief foray into the digital world was just idle curiosity, but the computer would be a more serious consideration when I finished my master's degree. A master's degree in music composition was completely worthless in terms of obtaining employment. Only a doctorate would gain one entry into the ranks of the professors in any university of standing.

Faced with imminent unemployment, I responded to a call from IBM to come to Kansas City and take an aptitude test to become a programmer or systems analyst for the burgeoning computer industry. In the days before academic degrees were offered in computer science, IBM selected young people of promise and trained them themselves. Music students were in particular demand because the company had discovered that there was a positive correlation between music training and computer programming. I traveled to Kansas City and took a series of tests, followed by several interviews. Returning home I waited for the results. When a week or more had passed without any word from IBM I panicked and went to the placement office in the school of education to see what might be available in the way of public-school teaching jobs.

There was a job opening in the Four-Corners region of Colorado and I gave the school superintendent a call. He offered the position to me on the phone, but I said that I would need to come out and take a look at the place before I would sign a contract. I spent the next day driving out to Dolores, Colorado, and a second day looking over the school. Everyone was very congenial and I found the mountain scenery breathtaking. By the end of the day I had signed a contract and called home to inform my wife. She informed me that IBM had called and they were offering me a position as a systems analyst, which would include a year of training at full salary.

Suddenly I was faced with what turned out to be the most important decision of my life. Rather than spend any time deliberating it, I impulsively said that I had already signed a contract and I would honor it. I called IBM and thanked them for their kind offer and prepared to move out to Colorado to begin work as the only music teacher in the town. It seemed that the die was cast and that music had won out over technology for once and for all. That proved not to be the case, but that momentary decision determined my career path for the future.

Music and Technology IV

Michigan State University

One year of teaching music in the public schools in Dolores, Colorado, convinced me that public-school teaching was not a good long-term occupation for me. I applied to the University of Michigan and Michigan State University schools of music for their Ph.D. programs in music composition. Having been accepted at both, I chose Michigan State because their offer of graduate teaching assistantship support was better.

We moved to East Lansing, Michigan, and I got settled into the School of Music as a graduate assistant in music theory. At Michigan State I chose Dr. H. Owen Reed, a Midwestern regional composer of distinction, as my composition teacher. My work in music theory was under the direction of Dr. Paul Harder, who was working on teaching materials for the first two years of music-theory instruction using a then-revolutionary approach called programmed instruction. This was a paper-and-pencil version of what would, in later years, become computer-assisted instruction. Again, I was not far from technology.

When it came time to fulfill the Ph.D. requirement of two foreign languages I petitioned the university to allow me to study computer programming as a substitute for one of the languages. After considerable controversy, the request was granted and I became the first of many future Ph.D. students who chose computer science as a substitute for one of the foreign language requirements. I proposed to take the full undergraduate sequence in computer science as my fulfillment of the German language requirement. That sequence was three courses in length, which was all the undergraduate computer-science courses that Michigan State offered at the time. The courses included programming languages and computer architecture. While I was learning programming I wrote several programs to test music-theory principles and a program to output all combinatorial 12-tone rows.

Near the end of my graduate studies at MSU I flew to St. Louis to attend the Music Teachers National Conference annual convention with Dr. Harder and several other graduate students. I was walking through the exhibits area when I saw a young man sitting at a booth with a strange-looking high tech gadget behind him. No one was stopping by to find out what he was showing, so I stopped and introduced myself. He was Robert Moog and the gadget behind him was the music synthesizer that he had just invented. He had taped versions of what would become the best-selling album "Switched On Bach" by Walter Carlos that had just been created using the Moog Synthesizer. I was intrigued and spent the next hour or so learning the basics of music synthesis from this pioneer figure in the field. Music and technology were coming closer and closer together.

Music and Technology V

Iowa State University

When I finished coursework for my doctorate and had the dissertation, which was a symphony, well underway, I began looking for college-level teaching positions. The year was 1967, which was a very fortunate year in terms of getting a university position. The baby boomers were beginning to arrive at college age and enrollments were rising rapidly. Colleges and universities all over the U.S. were desperate for new faculty to meet the demand. Young people coming out of Ph.D. programs at that time had many choices of academic employment.

After looking over the openings I decided to apply to the University of Michigan and Iowa State University. U. of M. is a major university with graduate degrees in music through the Ph.D. Locating there would give me a career with potential for national recognition in the field. Iowa State University, on the other hand, was just starting an undergraduate degree in music, and they were wanting someone to head up their music-theory program. This would give me the opportunity, right out of graduate school, to design and implement my own curriculum. I was offered both positions and decided on Iowa State, mostly due to the exciting opportunity to design my own curriculum. I was not disappointed. Iowa State provided me with leadership opportunities right from the beginning, and I enjoyed being a part of a growing music department. I went there thinking that I might spend five or so years and then move on, but I was very quickly tenured and reached full professor in less than ten years. I was priced out of the market; when I looked at positions at other universities they would have required a decrease in both academic rank and salary. I was at Iowa State for the long haul.

Once I had the music theory and music composition curricula well established I began to think about the rapidly growing field of electronic music. With my background in computers and interest in the new synthesizers I began to plan a unique computerized electronic-music studio for Iowa State. The National Endowment for the Humanities was offering summer institutes for college professors who wanted to enter the electronic music field and I applied for an institute at Dartmouth College and The University of New Hampshire. This institute, which was held on two successive summers, put me in contact with the leaders in this new field. I came home to Iowa State and put together a research proposal for the establishment of a computerized electronic-music studio. The proposal was funded, and I gathered two colleagues, a professor from the Electrical Engineering Department and an assistant professor from the Computer Science Department, and we began planning the Iowa State MUsic Studio (ISMUS), which was housed in the Computer Science building. Undergraduate and graduate students began to flood in, wanting to be a part of this unique opportunity. Over the next few years we graduated electrical engineers, computer scientists, and musicians with background in all three areas.

My career as a researcher lasted about five years. The development of MIDI systems, which led to the domination of the electronic music field by inexpensive Japanese keyboards, put an end to our research. One could simply purchase very powerful music synthesis systems at the local WalMart store, and larger systems were commercially available for serious musicians.

When we built a new music building at Iowa State I was in charge of working with the architects and acoustic designers for planning the new facility, which included a state-of-the-art electronic music and recording studio. That studio continues in operation to this day and I hope it is serving Iowa State well. After another ten years I moved out of leadership in that area and other younger faculty took over. My long years of combining music and technology were over, and I became just a consumer of the technology, much like many others who use the computer every day without thinking of the years and years of development that lay behind it.

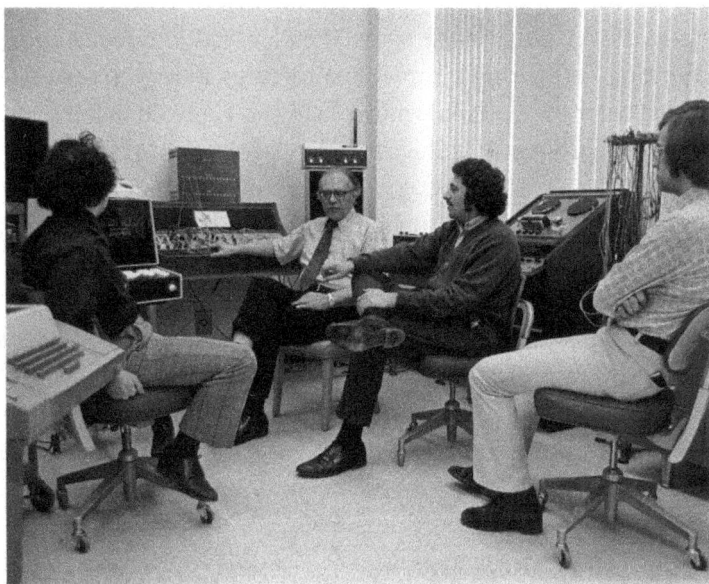

The ISMUS group hosting electronic music pioneer, Vladimir Ussechevsky (second from the left).

Milestones

There are events that stand out in my memory so starkly that I know exactly what I was doing at that moment. These are moments when I sensed that we were in for permanent change due to the epic nature of the events.

It is April 12, 1945, and I am sitting on the floor of our living room across the street from the telephone office in Cedar Vale, Kansas, listening to the radio. A news flash interrupts the music programming to inform me and the world that President Roosevelt has died. Since he has been president for my entire life, I don't know what to think. Is this the end of the world? No, things pretty much go on with little change and the event fades into history.

On November 22, 1963, my high-school choir from Dolores, Colorado, is in Cortez, Colorado, rehearsing for a massed choir festival to be held in the evening. We take a break for lunch and the news is relayed to us that President Kennedy has been shot. All the directors get together to decide what we are going to do: should we continue rehearsing and go on with the concert? Should we all go home and reschedule the event for some time later? If so, when? There is a lot of discussion about the difficulties of finding another time in all the various high-school schedules and some sentiment for simply going ahead. However, the consensus develops that we will postpone the performance to some future time. We simply can't think of going on after the event in Dallas. Of course, it is impossible to reschedule and that choir festival never happens. Is this the end of an era? How will the world change from that moment in time? Well, change it does, but not catastrophically. The event, however, doesn't fade into history and questions continue to be raised about what happened that day in Dallas, Texas. But our lives settle back into their usual routine and little changes from day to day.

It is September 11, 2001, and my daughter and her partner are visiting us in Boulder, Colorado. They are sleeping late and I am on the computer looking at the morning news. I read about the first plane flying into the World Trade Center tower and run immediately to turn on the television. Elyn and I are watching the event live when the second plane impacts the other tower and we continue to watch as the towers begin to fall. By that time my daughter is up and I tell her that this is truly the end of an era and that our individual and collective futures will be different than before that morning. So far, that prediction has proven accurate. I am reminded of the current "threat" level every time I go to an airport to fly. I have to take off my shoes to go through security and have my luggage opened and pawed through by strangers. Our country has entered into a protracted war that has drained our human and material resources. Only time will tell if my prediction of the end of an era will prove true.

Other events are not so easy to pinpoint. Where was I on the day that global warming started? Where were you on the day that the delicate balance that must be sustained for us humans to survive on this planet was irreversibly tipped? Or has that day not happened yet? Now *that* is a milestone to watch for.

The CVHS Yearbook

When I was a junior at Cedar Vale Memorial High School I was offered a position on the yearbook staff. Having successfully completed Mr. Jewell's typing class gave me all the qualifications I needed. Our business teacher, Mr. Jewell, was a tallish man with a beak-like nose and the wildest comb-over I had ever seen. Around and around and back and forth went his remaining strands of hair, all in the vain attempt to hide the inevitable. Mr. Jewell wasn't fooling anyone, but he was making a valiant effort.

My motives for joining the yearbook staff were pretty simple— there were many more girls than boys on the staff, and that position gave me the opportunity to socialize with girls in the evenings in a deserted school building relatively unsupervised. Also, it was enticing to be able to influence what was said about me and my classmates in a permanent printed document.

We met several evenings each week and poured over mountains of photographs and pages of copy to meet the deadline for publication. The form of the layout was typewritten copy and photo cutouts pasted on sheets provided by the yearbook printer. The printer also supplied some standard artwork that we could cut out and paste on the pages. The desks at the back of the business classroom were piled high with all our stuff and the smell of rubber cement was thick in the air. Far from being all work, I remember taking rest breaks with various girls in darkened hallways and even the gymnasium below. It was like being on a date without the need to pay for refreshments.

Heated discussions were a nightly occurrence as we tried to create a memento of our school year that was accurate, interesting, and a little "spicy." Sometimes staff members would read pages created by other staff members that were a little too revealing for their tastes, and feelings would run high. Mr. Jewell presided over all this chaos with good humor, a sure hand as to how much we could get by the school administration, and with a modicum of good taste. Of course, those students who were not on the staff, or did not have friends on the staff, had absolutely no say about what was put in the book. We were all aware of this power and secretly reveled in it.

Much of the book was pretty routine—photos of each student, group shots of all the clubs, musical organizations, sports teams, etc., but then there were header sections before all that stuff and several sections for candid shots around the school. Those sections were the most fun to put together, and we all vied for the cleverest one-liners to put on the photo cutouts in those sections.

The yearbook was supported by local businesses, and we sold ads and carefully set them up to meet the requirements of our advertisers. We were all quite proud of the results, which were available for purchase by students near the end of the school year. I remember the day when we all got our yearbooks and took turns autographing our photos in each other's yearbooks.

Having now written and published dozens of books, I can say that being on the CVHS yearbooks staff was one of my more important educational experiences in Cedar Vale High School. That goes to show that education appears in many forms, even when we least expect it and when our motivation may be just to socialize with the girls.

Effie Foster

An email brings me a picture of Effie Foster, our sixth-grade teacher at Cedar Vale grade school. This picture was taken on the occasion of her 100th birthday. What memories come flooding back when I see that familiar face!

We had a lot of good teachers during our years in the Cedar Vale public schools. Just consider the accomplishments of our little class of thirty-five students. Of all the teachers I had, however, Mrs. Foster was the most distinctive. It was clear to me that Mrs. Foster was living a passionate life. She approached everything she did with verve and heart. When she read us *Uncle Tom's Cabin*, Mrs. Foster openly wept at the sad chapters. When discipline was necessary, Mrs. Foster had fire in her eyes. Every lesson was a new adventure for her—and for us. Mrs. Foster was a big, raw-boned farm woman who was a force of nature.

The sixth-grade classroom at Cedar Vale grade school also served as the school library. Mrs. Foster was the librarian for the whole school. She encouraged me to devour as many books in that library as I could. The library collection was not regularly expanded, and most of the books were antiques even at that time. That library would bring a pretty sum today if it was sold on eBay. I would finish my lessons before some of my classmates and walk to the back of the room to peruse the stacks. To call them stacks is a slight exaggeration because there were only three or four floor-to-ceiling bookshelves in the library, and part of those were devoted to younger children's books. I think I pulled down and looked at every book on those shelves during my sixth-grade year, and some I read from cover to cover.

Mrs. Foster had fiery red hair that matched her disposition. She was hardly a model of femininity. In fact, she took little note of details of her appearance. My mother related a story about Bob Hays talking with his mother, Flo. It seems that Bob, who was always aware of the details of his surroundings, asked his mother, "Mom, would it be all right for me to tell Mrs. Foster when her underskirt is showing?" "Oh, my, no, Bob, Mrs. Foster's slip has been showing for years. Just ignore it."

Mrs. Foster presided over a group of children who were on their way to becoming adults. Hormones were running high and boys and girls were beginning to take a new interest in each other. Mrs. Foster took all this as a matter of course and dealt with it head on, just as she did everything else. She was, in short, the perfect teacher at the perfect time in my life. I left the sixth grade a very different and more mature person than I was coming in. I can't thank Mrs. Foster enough for her wonderful, blunt approach to teaching and to life.

Mother Unknown

The history of my father's family is filled with dead ends. As much as I have tried to research it, I can only get a few generations back. I am also in a somewhat unique position in that family. My father had one brother, Vernon, and two sisters, Fern and Sylvia. Fern never married and the other two siblings had no children, leaving me the only grandchild of my paternal grandparents.

One day in about 2000 I was visiting with Sylvia Smith, my one remaining aunt on my father's side (my father and the other two siblings having already died) at her residence in the nursing home in Sedan, Kansas. We were talking about our family when Sylvia suddenly made the following startling pronouncement in her inimitable Kansas farm-woman style: "You know, we have Indian blood in the family. . . . (whispering) but I'm not ashamed of it!" Well, that is the first I had heard of it, although my father and his siblings must have known all along! Sylvia proceeded to tell me what she knew about this Indian ancestor and I took careful note of what she described.

As soon as I could do so, I began to search the records and, sure enough, there in a birth record for my great-great-grandmother was the notation: "Mother unknown." The father, John Wheeler, born in 1792 in England, was carefully noted, along with the vital statistics for my great-great-grandmother, Mary Elizabeth Wheeler, born 9 April 1826 in Bellefontaine, Ohio. How, I ask you, could the name of the father and child be known, but not the mother? As many ways as I have tried to search out the records for this great-great-great-grandmother, she remains a mystery. I do know that she was a Native American because Sylvia had described to me exactly where I would find her.

Now that I know of our Native American heritage I look at my grandmother's face in family pictures and clearly see the facial characteristics of her Indian heritage. That nothing had been said to me in all those years speaks volumes about how Native American heritage was viewed in the early twentieth century in our little corner of Kansas. That Sylvia had to whisper conspiratorially that she wasn't ashamed also speaks volumes.

I, on the other hand, am proudly 1/32nd Native American and I think of my great-great-great-grandmother quite often with love and affection whoever she might have been. It may only be a romantic fantasy, but when I visit the Native American pueblos in my area of New Mexico and hear the drums and witness the dancing, I feel a subtle trilling in my veins. I like to think that it is my great-great-great-grandmother coming back to enjoy the drumming. I am proud to carry her blood and happy to send it along to the coming generations. Nothing is ever lost in this human family, so long as we choose to remember. If we choose to forget, we all lose.

Picking Up the Pieces

As a youngster growing up in Cedar Vale, Kansas, I was like a fish out of water. Most people around me were focused on their immediate surroundings while I seemed to always have my eye somewhere out beyond the horizon. I was called a hopeless dreamer by some members of my family, and they probably despaired of my ever "making a go of it" in the "real" world. The people that I was attracted to were those who had "been out there" and done things, or at least had dreamed of doing things. I believed that Bill Leonard had been a circus musician (see "Leonard Theater, Cedar Vale, Kansas," p. 1). Mrs. Walker (see "The Whitney Drug Store," p. 36) was quite a "dime-store" philosopher. Mrs. Kirby (see "Bertha Kirby," p. 112) lived in an imaginary world of piano music, barely touching down to earth long enough to make it to the next lesson. To those who focused on the ground we were actually standing on, all of us dreamers must have been incomprehensible. We were the "weird ducks" who were barely tolerated but didn't really count for much.

As soon as I could, I dusted Cedar Vale off my feet and didn't look back. As much as possible, I avoided even thinking about the first eighteen years of my life. As I began to achieve success in the larger world it was very easy to keep that early part of my life in a tightly sealed box that was never opened. I was living in the world of my imagination and making a good living doing so. I was proud that I had done what my family thought was impossible and been recognized for it. I well remember years later, when I would visit my first wife's parents in northern Kansas, my father-in-law, a retired farmer, would ask me what I planned to do when my current job "ran out." (I was a tenured professor of music at the time.) There was nothing I could say that would convince to him that my current job was unlikely to ever run out. My professional life was beyond his comprehension. If I had visited Cedar Vale in those years I'm sure I would have been met with similar attitudes.

As my professional achievements grew I began to have a sense of internal discontinuity. I seemed to be divided into several parts that didn't really fit together. There was the "me" that had a growing national and international recognition as a composer, author, and college professor, coexisting with a "me" that had lived through considerable ridicule and abuse as a young person. There was even a "me" that was a counter-culture hippy, while another "me" was raising a family as a respected member of a university community. That I managed to keep all this within one body without losing my health is a tribute to the solid genes of my peasant background and a good intuition about what would have put me completely over the edge.

Now, in my maturity, I see my task as self integration—putting all the pieces together. With some professional help and the patience of those near and dear to me I am breaking down the barriers among my various selves. A significant part of my process is revisiting my early years in Cedar Vale and sharing the memories with you, my reader. I am enjoying trying to remember just what was in each building on the main street of Cedar Vale and many memories of the details of my young life keep flooding to the surface as I do so.

The Junior/Senior Prom

When I was a junior at Cedar Vale High School we held our junior/senior prom in the band room on the second floor of the old Bonnell building, which the schools had taken over for FFA, the manual arts shop, and a bus barn. We reached the second floor of this building by climbing a small covered stairway on the south side. These stairs were in a narrow, dark passageway between two adjacent buildings.

It was the junior class's responsibility to decorate the hall for the prom. I don't remember what the theme was, but we had lots of crêpe-paper streamers that we twisted and put up across the space. My clearest memory of that evening was that I had a stapler open to staple crêpe paper to the walls and window frames. Judy Huddle was working with me on that project and on a sudden impulse, I put the stapler against her upper arm and clicked off a staple. It penetrated her arm and stuck there. We were both shocked and I quickly extracted the missile, which left just two tiny dots of blood. I don't know which of us was more horrified. I had dated Judy, either before or after this incident, though I am inclined to think that it must have been before. I don't know if she would have dated me afterwards! Anyway, that incident stuck in my memory just as the staple stuck in Judy's arm.

We finished the job and the band room was completely transformed, I think into some sort of South Seas island. The next evening we had a banquet in the school cafeteria, which was also decorated, followed by a dance in the South Seas island ambience of the band room. We had hired a live band for the evening and everyone was dressed to the nines. The costume for such events was a suit and tie for the boys and a strapless evening gown with lots of stiff mesh gathered into rosettes at the bodice and all over the skirt for the girls.

My date for the evening was a senior girl, Marilyn Holroyd. She was a Church of Christ member and not allowed to dance. Nevertheless, we enjoyed the refreshments and listened to the music. Not being able to dance was not a disappointment to me since I had a fair amount of experience playing in dance bands but absolutely no experience dancing. I considered her to be a friend and had no romantic intentions toward her. We simply enjoyed each other's company for the evening and I drove her home. I do remember thinking that she was quite beautiful in her evening gown for the prom.

At the time the whole event seemed quite posh and glamorous to me. I thought we had done an amazing job of creating beautiful decorations for the enjoyment of the graduating class.

In recent months I've learned that Judy Huddle/French has had a series of knee replacements and Marilyn Holroyd/Wilkinson has suffered a stroke, a sign that none of us are the teens we were when these events occurred. I am happy to report that both are recovering nicely at this writing.

Publishing

One day in the year 2000 my wife and partner, Elyn, returned from a pilgrimage conference and said, "They want to be able to buy my book, but it is out of print." Elyn had written the first modern account of an American pilgrim on the Camino de Santiago in Spain. The Camino had been the subject of Elyn's Ph.D. dissertation from Princeton, and the book, *Following the Milky Way*, had been written several years later and published by Iowa State University Press. As is true of most publishers, the press had produced one print run and then dropped the project, giving the copyright back to Elyn.

Well, I had spent the last thirteen years or so designing and laying out books, so my response was, "Let's publish it!" Of course, being a publisher is considerably more involved than being a pager for a major publisher. I had to learn about the ins and outs of ISBN numbers, registering with the Library of Congress, as well as the distribution network that assures that books actually reach the market. It was, in short, a project right down my alley. We decided to leave the interior of *Following the Milky Way* as it was in the first edition but to add a new introduction for a second edition.

In the next few months I learned all I could about the publishing business and set up Pilgrims Process, Inc., publishers. *Milky Way* came out in 2001, along with a mystery, *Dead End on the Camino,* that Elyn had written several years before. Since the mystery was also set on the Camino we thought the two books would go well together. That was the beginning of our publishing venture, and it wasn't long before other projects were being proposed to us.

I have said that Pilgrims Process is a niche publisher. We publish books that other, larger publishers will not take on, and our subject matter is limited to whatever intrigues and interests me. Since I have no desire to earn significant income from publishing we can publish books that will be best sellers with an audience of a few hundred people. The book you are holding is one of our projects. Our catalog is over twenty books and the subject matter is wildly varied, as you can see by visiting our web site at www.pilgrimsprocess.com.

I receive a steady stream of proposals for books but take on very few projects. A book has to intrigue me for me to put out the effort to publish it. This book is the first of my own writing that we have published, and I rather think it will be the last.

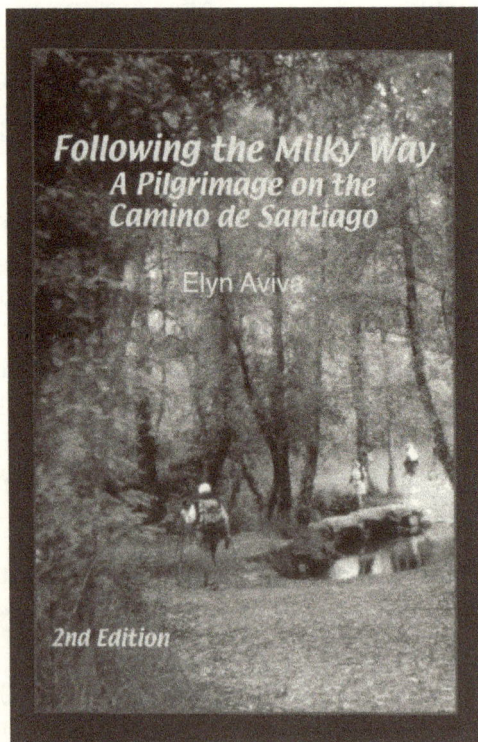

Following the Milky Way
A Pilgrimage on the
Camino de Santiago

Elyn Aviva

2nd Edition

A Ghost Story

It is the 1959-60 school year and I am teaching in the public schools of Hoxie, Kansas. I have spent the weekend back at KU where my fiance is attending college. It is the early morning, before dawn, on a Monday, and I am driving straight through to Hoxie to be there in time to conduct the morning band rehearsal at 8:00 a.m. I often make this night-time journey and then catch up on sleep during the week. (There isn't much for a single teacher to do in Hoxie.)

I am driving the interstate out across the plains west of Salina, Kansas, and the land stretches out flat as far as I can see in every direction. The eastern sky is just beginning to show yellows and reds and the landscape begins to appear around me. I am driving at least 60 miles per hour in my old Pontiac when I look off to the north out the passenger window. What I see there makes my hair stand straight up on end. Outside the window are the head and shoulders of a man who seems to be riding right along with me and looking straight at me. Thinking it must be my own reflection in the glass, I blink my eyes several times but he doesn't go away.

I would describe him as being older than middle age, nearly bald, with tufts of hair sticking out from his head in several places. His complexion is dark, almost orange, and his eyes are piercing and bloodshot. I stare at him as long as I can stand it and then just look straight down the road, hoping to find a place where I can stop. I absolutely do not want to stop in the middle of open country with this guy looking in the window at me. I don't know exactly how long I drive like this in utter terror, but I see a gas station on the side of the road ahead and it looks open. I pull in and see a little truck stop café that is also open. Being careful not to look out the right-hand car window, I get out and go into the café. I drink several cups of strong coffee with shaking hands and eat a good breakfast. After about a half hour I go back to my car. The sun is up and the sky is blue. Now I finally can look at the right side of the car. There is nothing there.

Getting back into my car, I complete my trip to Hoxie in time to change clothes and hurry to the band rehearsal. What a relief to be back in familiar surroundings, with kids acting up and talking the way kids do. I want to hug them all this morning.

It is several years before I can tell this story and this is the first time I have written it all down. Just writing it gives me a little chill up the back of my neck.

The Commies Are Coming!

In the heady days after the end of World War II we have a new enemy on the horizon—Communism. Those Russkies are vowing to eat us for breakfast and we are afraid of their nuclear weapons, but even more so, we are afraid of a silent invasion of communist cells forming in our midst. Guardians of our freedom and way of life such as Senator Joseph McCarthy are looking under every bed in Washington, DC, and Hollywood for commie cells.

Where were HUAC, the CIA, the FBI, and the whole alphabet soup in the 1870s when Cedar Vale was home to not one but *three* communist cells? Not the geeks who looked through the wastebaskets in Washington, or the debauched artists in Hollywood, but real, living, breathing Russians in cells just a few miles outside of Cedar Vale—my own home town.

They entered the U.S. under assumed names. Vladimir Konstantinovich Geins became William Frey and his wife, Maria Slavinskaya, became Mary Frey. They entered the U.S. in 1868 and in New York City they met other future members of the Cedar Vale cell. A Russian couple named Ponofiloff, who entered under the name of Brook, were to become founders of the first Cedar Vale cell. They travelled on very different paths to arrive in Chautauqua County without raising suspicion of the authorities. They formed the Progressive Community and started a newspaper. In a few years the Investigative Community had been formed, and a few years later another group from Russia had formed a third community. It looked like freedom and democracy and our way of life were soon going to be a thing of the past.

Are you wondering why we were able to grow up in CV without being ruled by communist dictators? Well, one thing those commies hadn't figured on was Kansas weather! They nearly died of frostbite the first winter, before they constructed adequate housing. The land was very hard to break out and they were not well equipped for the task since they were not Russian peasants but members of the intelligentsia who had absolutely no experience in farming or building houses. By 1880 the whole bubble was over without military intervention or even a single hearing by the HUAC. What a relief!

Thought question for today: How many offices in the current Department of Homeland Security are devoted to protecting us from the communist threat?

Cedar Vale Miniature Village

I remember in my youth in Cedar Vale, Kansas, that there was a house in my neighborhood in the southwestern corner of the town with the most unusual feature. The house was not remarkable but the yard was unlike anything I had seen. It was filled to the brim with miniature houses, all lined up in neat rows and identified by the name of the owner. This was the home of Frank and Ida Zimmerman, a couple in their 80s. Frank, it seems, was the master carpenter who had built all these houses. There was a high hedge all around the house so that we had to enter through the front gate. Just inside the gate was a box for paying admission to the village, which represented Cedar Vale in the 1930s or even earlier. The Zimmermans were always on hand to give us a guided tour and point out all the buildings that we knew and to talk about them. After the tour, there was usually some refreshment that Ida had prepared for us. They always seemed very happy to spend some time with any of the kids in the neighborhood.

The garage was as unusual as the yard. It was covered with old license plates, mostly from Chautauqua County, Kansas. Inside the garage was Frank's workshop and a very old wooden school bus. It seems that Frank had built the school bus in the 1920s and used it to haul children to school for many years. The 1930 Federal Census lists Frank's occupation as "Bus Driver—School Bus." Perhaps his long experience with children accounted for the warm welcome we all received in visiting their little museum of Cedar Vale's past. I never thought about what their motivation might have been for being so generous with their time. Now I rather think that they were interested in preserving some of the history of the town and educating us kids about that history.

The miniature village ceased to exist when the Mrs. Zimmerman passed away. Frank went to Sedan, where he died September 1, 1958, at the age of ninety. Many of the original houses in the miniature village now reside in the Cedar Vale Museum where another generation of young people can admire them.

Jay D. Mills

Having Fun

Recently, Elyn and I met with a financial planner to help us better allocate our assets and insure that we continue to be able to do everything we want to do and have enough money to last us the rest of our lives. If you are in the over-sixty age bracket and haven't done so, I highly recommend this process if you can find someone who isn't just selling a financial product. I am willing to pay for advice but resent wasting my time listening to a sales spiel.

The planner conducted a lengthy interview and ended by asking a series of questions about what money means to each of us. His questions probed deeper and deeper until we reached the rock bottom of what money means in our lives. I quickly moved through "having financial security" and the desire not to have to spend my time thinking about money, to my rock-bottom response, which was: "I want to have the freedom to have fun in my life." Having fun for me means comfortable surroundings, good friends, travel to interesting places, eating good food, giving and receiving body work, maintaining my health, doing regular spiritual practice, and having time to do projects that are interesting to me and also time to just sit and vegetate. Interesting projects to me are projects like writing this book, starting a blog for high-school classmates, publishing a book or so each year— all of which are free of any profit motive. That is now my goal in life.

I was asked by the planner how long I expected to live and we agreed on a number of ninety years. So, in a nutshell, I intend to live a life that is interesting and nourishing to me along the lines outlined above. I want to have the good health to do most of those things for as long as I live, even up to ninety years of age, and to have a good and peaceful death. That's what I mean by having fun! I face the future with a smile on my face. Every day is a new adventure.

My computer monitor now has a sign posted on its frame: "But, will it be FUN?"

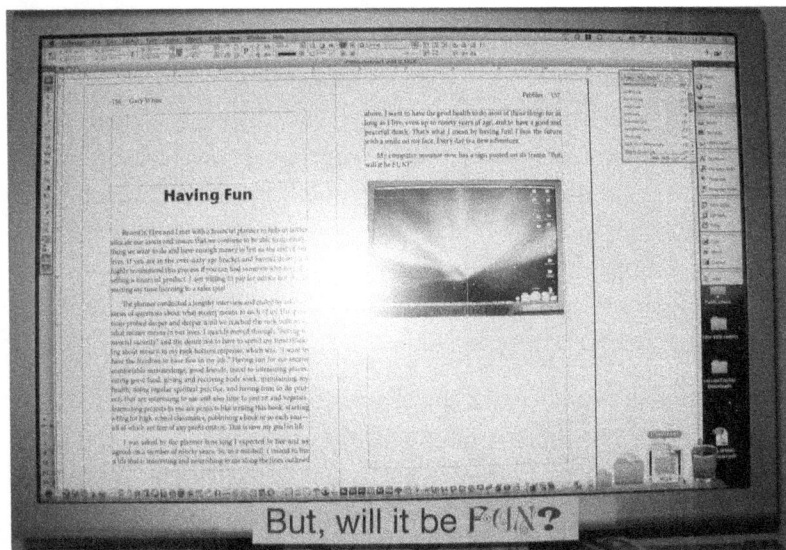

Swimming

My mother never learned to swim. She was deathly afraid of the water and passed the phobia on to me by constant admonitions to "not go near the water." This was a severe limitation on my summer fun since the local boys would gather at the swimming hole above the dam on the Caney river just outside of Cedar Vale, Kansas, for their afternoon dips. My father also never learned to swim, but he could dog paddle and was not as afraid of the water as my mother.

In an effort to overcome my fear, Dad bought me a face mask and snorkel that would allow me to go underwater and explore. He knew of a few swimming holes on Cedar Creek where the bottom was solid rock and the water usually crystal clear. The two of us started going to these swimming holes several afternoons each week. While at first I was petrified to put my head under water, I gradually was drawn to that underwater world by the sheer beauty I found there. I discovered that once I was totally submerged the sunfish were not afraid of me and would swim up and actually touch my body with curiosity. Watching reflected sunlight filtering through the surrounding trees and observing the underwater residents was endlessly fascinating, and I would spend as much time underwater as I could, just surfacing for air from time to time.

Needing to be able to get around underwater led to learning to dog paddle. Then I could even move across the swimming hole without the mask on my face. However, my fundamental fear of the water remained.

It was not until many years later, when I had children of my own, that I determined to not pass mother's phobia on to my own children. I went to the local swimming pool and took a beginning swimming class for adults. Finally, I learned to actually do the crawl stroke and, while swimming is not really enjoyable for me, at least I could swim with my own children and was happy that they took to the water with no fear and enjoyed swimming as they grew up.

The swimming hole on Caney river.

Three

I grew up in a household with three people, myself and my two parents. In some ways we were a close family and in other ways very distant. One dynamic in our family was a certain ambiguity in my mother's relationship with me. That there was some sexual content is undeniable. When I asked my mother about this in the last years of her life she simply said, "I didn't know much about sex." One expression of this ambiguity was the fact that I regularly slept with my parents until age ten or eleven. That this shaped me in a particular way only became apparent in my middle years.

During the period when "swinging" and "open marriage" was all the rage I had many opportunities to experience sexual threesomes and found that this pattern seemed both natural and ideal to me. You may wonder about the gender of the third party. Well, I had experiences with both combinations and found them equally satisfying. I could, at this point, go into specifics but that would lead us down the path to the erotic and I am determined not to go there. Sorry to disappoint some of my readers.

Needless to say, this sexual preference has created difficulties in both my marriages. I've worked it out in a variety of ways, but it is simply a fact of life that I live with every day. I've had therapists analyze my proclivity in several ways. One theory is that it is a way of avoiding the intimacy that a relationship between two people creates. Another theory is that there is a strong homosexual element in this preference. Some have placed the label "bisexual" on me and I have sometimes identified myself that way too. No theory that I have heard to date seems adequately to explain the pattern to me. My personal belief is that it is simply a pattern that was established early in my life and "as the twig is bent, so grows the tree."

So, in conclusion, I can say that I find a conversation among three people to be the most satisfying and natural, and that preference also extends to the bedroom.

In Megalithic Sites

I place my hand over your handprint and trace the spirals you painstakingly cut in the hardest stone you could find, without benefit of power tools. I wonder what messages you intended to send and what language you were writing. What did you see and experience deep in the caves and caverns you found or excavated all over the landscape of Europe and the British Isles? Did you see that the stones were entries into other realms? Were your spirals and zigzags the tracings of what you saw there—or were they just graffiti? "Harry + Sally—True Love," "Kilroy was here," "What I think, you will think,"—like these little pebbles I'm dredging up out of my own memories, worn smooth in the telling and retelling to myself and others?

This much I know: it was an insult for me to ever think of you as primitive and stupid. It was an insult to you and an insult to me because we are not such distant relatives, you and me. For me, whose feet have never truly known the earth and whose eyes have never truly mapped the sky, to look down on you whose knowledge of such things eclipses mine is the true stupidity. I freely acknowledge it to you now.

I have had the map of my own DNA drawn. I see my ancestral self moving slowly up out of Africa, through the Middle East, and across the map of Europe to finally leap to these shores just a few generations ago. Yes, you and me, we are one. Your flesh is my flesh. "We are family."

So I place my hand again over your handprint and say, "Hail and farewell, brother and sister." I think that a glimmer of understanding is beginning to develop in our collective consciousness here and in this time. We have all passed this way and will continue so long as the earth is hospitable to our species. Is that what you are trying to tell me? If so, I get the message, loud and clear.

Firebug!

When I was six or seven years old I was given a bunch of waterproof matches. They must have been "war surplus" because I remember also being given either K or C rations. Remember K rations? I just checked into them. Did you know that the K rations were manufactured by the makers of Cracker Jack™? Anyway, these fireproof matches could be soaked in water and they would light just as if they were dry. To my seven-year-old mind that was miraculous.

I remember showing one of my friends, perhaps Donna Burch, how these matches worked. We were playing at a ditch near our house, and I was dipping a match into the water in the ditch and then lighting it. I hit upon the idea of burning a little of the dry grass nearby, just to see what would happen. Well, the grass took off burning and I couldn't stop it. I ran home and my mother called the fire department to come and put out the blaze.

I felt sure that I would never be able to show my face again in Cedar Vale after such a crime. Embarrassment kept me at home for most of a day. When I finally went out with my dad to Clarence Marshall's service station I was greeted with, "There's the firebug!" The fire in the grass was nothing to the fire on my face. After that I was known as "firebug" for what seemed like a long time. Finally the joke played itself out and I wasn't reminded any more of my transgression. However, I never forgot the lesson about fire that I learned that day.

Time Machine

Do you remember the comic strip Alley Oop? It is still being drawn today. Dr. Elbert Wonmug had a time machine that brought Alley and all his friends into the twentieth century or twentieth-century folk back to the Stone Age. Far fetched you say? Wait a minute, friends.

Recently a classmate and I were blogging about one Judy G., a girl we both knew at the University of Kansas. In my memory, Judy G. still exists as a twenty-year-old beauty with a dewy complexion and a smile that is stunning. Then my classmate wrote about "little Nadine Foster." Four-year-old Nadine came clearly into my memory just as I last saw her—no bigger than a minute and faster than greased lightning. Other classmates remain just as they were when I last saw them, even though they must be in their 60s or 70s by now. Our time machine is our memories, and that's why I have so much fun bringing the past back into the present and enjoying it again. So, keep your own time machine going—Dr. Wonmug has nothing on us!

Index